Pride
vs
Prejudice

by
Bishan Dass Bains

First published in Great Britain in 2015
by Bishan Dass Bains

A CIP catalogue record for this
book is available from the British Library

ISBN 978-0-9575238

INDEX

FOREWORD
by Professor Carl Chinn

In early 2013, the 'Express and Star' revealed that Wolverhampton has the second highest percentage of Sikh residents living in England. In total, nine per cent of the city's 249,500 residents regarded themselves as Sikh, according to data released from the 2011 census, with only Slough having a higher percentage. Sikhs are also prominent in Smethwick, Birmingham and elsewhere in the West Midlands and they play a key role in the economic, social and cultural life of our region – as do Hindus.

Their population in Wolverhampton is also higher than the England and Wales average, standing just under 4%. Many Hindus originate from Gujarat but came to the West Midlands in the 1970s from Uganda and Kenya, where they had been settled for decades. However, like the Sikhs, other Hindus trace their roots to the Punjab.

Although there were a few score Indians in the West Midlands in the 1920s and 1930s, there was no large-scale movement of Sikhs and Hindus here. But following the Second World War, the 1948 British Nationality Act guaranteed free right of entry to British subjects and Commonwealth Citizens. For much of the 1950s, it was mostly men and women from the West Indies who took advantage of this opportunity and as late as 1954 there were just ten Indian families living in Wolverhampton.

Slowly that number increased and within two years the newly-formed Indian Workers Association in the town had a membership of 150; whilst by the end of the decade the number of

South Asian people locally had risen to 1,756. But it was during the 1960s that there was a marked increase in immigration to the West Midlands from India and Pakistan.

At first many of the newcomers were single Sikh and Hindu men from the villages close to the city of Jalandhar in the Punjab. They came to join the pioneers from their villages who had already established themselves and who had become the first links in a chain of migration. It was they who provided a base, support and advice for newcomers. These hard-working young Indians played a vital role in the rebuilding of a war-ravaged Britain, settling in the Dudley Road and Blakenhall areas of Wolverhampton, in Caldmore in Walsall, and in and around Smethwick town centre and its Cape Hill area.

Wherever they lived, Indian immigrants faced difficult conditions. Large Victorian houses were turned into lodging houses, sleeping sometimes as many as fifteen or sixteen friends or members of an extended family. Rent was about ten shillings a week, on top of which £1 10s was paid weekly into a community ration for food.

Those in work helped those who had not yet found a job, but in the 1950s and early 1960s there was plenty of employment – albeit immigrants found it all but impossible to get skilled work because of discrimination or a lack of knowledge in English. Across the Black Country, then, many Indian men went into labouring jobs in the foundries. It was hard, dirty, dusty and thirsty work.

One of the pioneers of this Indian migration was Bishan Dass Bains, whose absorbing and inspirational life story has been set down in an important book called 'Pride v Prejudice'.

It is important because it is a rare account of a first-generation immigrant's experiences. In particular his story of aspiration, endeavour and achievement is reflected in the stories of so many of the Hindus and Sikhs of Wolverhampton, Walsall, Smethwick, Birmingham and elsewhere. Today many of the sons and daughters, grandsons and granddaughters of those early Indian immigrants are prosperous in business, or else they have moved into the professions, becoming solicitors, accountants, doctors, and chemists amongst others. They are valuable and valued citizens.

But the story of Bishan Dass Bains has another importance, one which is more specific to him as a man and as a citizen. This is   because his life highlights his constant battle against prejudice and for equality. From his childhood in the Punjab to his working and political life in Wolverhampton, Bishan Dass Bains has proudly striven for the cause of making a better, fairer and more tolerant society. He is a man to be admired and he is a man both Wolverhampton and the Punjab should be proud for his achievements and for his ongoing fight against prejudice.

I would like to acknowledge with grateful thanks the co-operation of the Express & Star in giving kind permission to reproduce the press cuttings in this book.

INTRODUCTION

Wolverhampton is a vibrant multi-cultural and multi-racial city with a history that stretches back to 985AD. In 994 King Aethelred granted Title Deed of land known as the Heatune to Lady Wulfruna and she founded a church with a monastery which grew larger over the years. The town was named Wulfrunnas Heanton after her and later this changed to Wolverhampton. During Medieval and Tudor times Wolverhampton was popular as a wool town and was a major centre for the wool industry. During the industrial revolution the town became major centre important for the mining of iron ore, coal, limestone before subsequently became a centre for producing locks and keys, motorcycles and cars. The city was recently a major industrial centre in engineering, aerospace and cars. It was granted the status of Municipal Borough on 15th March 1848 and of County Borough of Staffordshire in 1889. In 1974 Wolverhampton became a Metropolitan Borough council and the Queen granted it city status in 2000.

After the First World War the huge shortage of housing gave rise to mass council housing development all over the borough. Today the city centre has popular modern shopping centres in the Beatties, Mander and Wulfrun centres and Wolverhampton University, next to the Civic Centre, has more than 24000 students coming from all over the world. The city is linked by a reasonable network of transport by roads, rail and tram which provide an easy link with other towns and city of Birmingham. According to the 2011 census the population of the city has grown to 251,462 of which 36% are from ethnic minorities, reflecting the rich diversity of people within the city. The City of Wolverhampton is now a fully fledged multi-ethnic and multi-cultural society than fifty spoken languages regularly used by its citizens. Undoubtedly it is now a much better place to live and work compared with before. I am proud to be associated with and to be living in this city over the last more than half a century. I regard myself a true Wulfrunian as against an Asian as I lived in India for only twenty one years of my early life.

This is the story of my time here in the West Midlands, from my arrival on a cold November evening in 1963, through my political career which took me to the high position of Mayor of Wolverhampton , to my decision to retire from active politics. Whilst it is an intensely personal journey I sincerely hope that this is the one from which other people may take inspiration

BACKGROUND

To fully understand the background to my story it is worth spending just a moment to put my time in India in the context of world affairs and the type of society into which I was born.

In the years from 1939 until 1945 the whole world was engulfed in Second World War, the darkest period in the history of human civilisation on this beautiful planet earth. The nations of the world had divided into two camps engaged in fighting a bloody war involving the butchery of humankind. An estimated 80/90 million people perished during the war, and among them many civilians who died not through bullets or bombs but through deliberate genocide, massacres, mass bombings, diseases and starvation. The Super Powers were engaged in establishing military might, political supremacy and the expansion of colonialism whilst subsequently small nations and weaker countries became embroiled in the evils of war against each other, even though they had neither intention nor interest in getting involved in this kind of barbaric act of human atrocities.

Whilst all this was happening, however, India was fighting for independence from Britain and the demand for home rule had already intensified and the War of Independence was reaching its peak. Under an agreement between the British government and Indian leaders, British India agreed to fight in the Second World War for Britain who in turn promised to grant home rule to India at the end of the war. After the conflict was over, however, the British government started drifting away from its promise to grant independence to India, which gave rise to a strong rebellion against British rule. There were up-rising rebellions amongst

3

Indian masses all over the country, demanding nothing less than what had been promised and to establish India as a democratic republic. In spite of all this, the future of the country was far from clear.

The Indian leaders representing the Indian masses were divided into many indigenous factions of castes, creeds, faiths and religions. The whole issue of independence was not a straight-forward or simple question to resolve—at the same time as looking at the national situation they were fighting their own corner to safeguard the rights of their respective communities and establish autonomous status. There was a great deal of mistrust prevailing amongst different sections of the community and their leaders. There were a great deal of scepticism amongst minorities of Hindu domination in free India, which subsequently resulted in division of the country into India and Pakistan.

The Indian leaders negotiating independence and home rule with the British government had some conflicting interests them-selves and hence divided in to different groups and factions. Some of them were keen to have political power transferred from white British to Indians whilst a second group of leaders were those who were fighting for social justice and equality of opportunity for all Indians in free India. They were striving for equal rights for all Indians in an independent India because they were fully aware that a large section of Indian population were denied basic human rights by their own compatriots over the past centuries.

A large section of the Indian population were classed as Untouchables who were scheduled castes and down-trodden. They were denied basic human rights and subjected to inhuman treatment over centuries. The so-called Untouchables saw no end to their humiliation and suffering at the hands of the upper caste Hindus. They had no right to education, could not buy land or other property, could not worship God, or even take drinking water from the same wells, and they were subjected to live in ghettoes like scavengers on the outskirts of the villages.

The circumstances and general environment influenced by the combination of the Second World War, the Indian War of Independence and the fight for equality for the Untouchables were bound to leave ever-lasting psychological scars upon any child born in those circumstances. A stigma of childhood always remains with a person for the rest of his life. There are millions who were born in poverty, brought up in poverty, educated or forced to remain illiterate in poverty, lived a life of poverty and in the end perished in poverty. The sorrows and suffering of millions throughout the world, deep rooted in deprivations and poverty often goes unnoticed by the rest of the world.

It was a historical struggle for dignity and equality. We are reminded of the milestone in 1927, when Baba Sahib B. R. Ambedkar along with his thousands of fellow marchers, protesters and people burned the most notorious law book well known by the name of 'The Manu Simitis'. This codified social laws that assigned permanent inferior status to the massive majority and then subjugated them under the hereditary rules of Varna and the caste system. This notorious law book assigns differential punish-ment to different castes for similar crimes. Therefore, this day is a great day in our life, when people who were left subjugated and oppressed under the social laws of Manu decided to burn the codes and conduct that made them lesser human beings—and all under the leadership of Baba Sahib Ambedkar the emancipator of down trodden masses of India.

5

India is a country of many denominations, faiths and religions which are further divided into hundred of castes and sub-castes. Although the country is rich with many natural resources and agricultural land, over the centuries - unfortunately - society remains infested with the stigma of caste and religious prejudice. People belonging to lower castes have long been deprived of basic human rights of equality, liberty and justice and the outside world is not fully aware of the extent and the gravity of the underlying deep-rooted problems of caste discrimination and prejudice in Indian society. The stigma of Untouchability remains with them wherever they went all over the world. The caste discrimination follows them as a calf follows a cow. Even if they attain higher qualifications, change profession and improve their financial and living standards the people belonging to lower castes are destined to born as Untouchables, live as Untouchables and eventually perish as Untouchables in spite of change of status. In other words, according to caste system an Untouchable - however superior he may be mentally and morally - is below a Touchable in rank who no matter how inferior he may be, will always rank above an Untouchable.

Discrimination of any kind is of course, bad and unacceptable in an advanced and civilized society of the 21st century but the caste prejudice is the worst kind of discrimination. Caste prejudice is not simply discrimination but a kind of guided notion deep-rooted in the human mind, which generates hatred amongst human beings belonging to the same religion. Those who practice racial discrimination or caste prejudice do not realise the grievous wounds they might be inflicting upon others. Many people of Indian origin living abroad still regard caste as a part of their lives and cultural heritage and proudly carry it with them wherever they go in the world. Discrimination and caste prejudice is still widely evident in the Indian community living abroad. Almost every Indian religious establishment and community organisation in United Kingdom and throughout the world is simply based upon different castes. It is regrettable that people belonging to the same denomination have different temple names to signify individual castes, thus socially segregating them from the rest of the community. The people from lower castes are still being looked upon in some way as being inferior to others and this attitude still transfers to future generations.

There have been numerous incidents of caste and religious prejudice in employment, social and cultural dealings in UK. It is worth mentioning the Tribunal case of The Hague Centre of Wolverhampton and J. Chandel & G. Sani V S. Pal & D. Bangay. In his 40 page judgment the tribunal judge highlighted very clear evidence of discrimination and prejudice having taken place in the name of religion and caste. In this book, I have mentioned several incidents of caste and racial prejudice in my personal and public life.

The Caste Watch Organisation in the UK has worked over the past many years to raise awareness regarding caste and religious discrimination. They have campaigned rigorously to outlaw caste discrimination (along with nine other inequalities) through the Single Equality Bill 2010. The Bill was introduced and proceeded through both Houses of Parliament in April 2014 but, unfortunately, the implementation has been put on hold due to political and pro-caste lobbying.

After Independence in 1947, India became a secular democratic republic and adopted a constitution which guaranteed basic human rights of equality, liberty and justice to all the citizens of the country. Over the years several new legislative measures passed by the Indian government designed to abolish untouchability and hatred based on caste and religion remain on the statue books due to a lack of will to implement them. It is ironic that the largest democracy of the world is flourishing well, yet is still supported by caste and religious segregation. Political leaders continue to exploit the secular status of a democratic country by begging votes based on castes and religion during elections.

Ravindera Nath Tagore, a great son of India, was awarded the Nobel Prize in Literature in 1913 and one of his famous poems written almost a century ago still reflects the prevailing circumstances of India:

Bring to this country once again the blessed name;
Which made the land of thy birth sacred to all distant lands?
Let thy great awakening under the Bodhi tree be fulfilled;
Let open the doors that are barred, and the resounding conch shell;
Proclaim thy arrival at Bharat's gate;
Let through innumerable voices, the gospel of an unmeasurable love announces thy call.

You can pass legislation to combat or reduce racial prejudice but despite that it is extremely difficult to eradicate the caste system. Racial prejudice may be more to do with race, colour, creed or politics but the caste prejudice is deep-rooted in religious beliefs - and you cannot introduce legislation to change people's religious beliefs. As Dr. B.R. Ambedkar has said, you cannot eradicate caste prejudice unless you destroy the notion that breeds the caste system. You cannot create a casteless society with out getting rid of those holy books and literature which breed the system and which inspire people to discriminate against their own compatriots

8

CHILDHOOD

I was born on 10th March 1942, in a small village called Shaffipur in the Jalandhar district of the Punjab in India. It was a secluded small village with a population of around 300 people. Like millions of villagers in rural India the inhabitants were largely illiterate and extremely orthodox. There were two main communities, Muslims and so-called Untouchables living in the village before the 1947 independence of India but during the partition into the separate countries of India and Pakistan, the Muslims went to Pakistan and their place taken over by Jat Sikhs coming over from Pakistan to India. They took over almost every-thing including houses, agricultural land and any property left behind by Muslim people. The attitude and general behaviour of newly arrived Jat Sikhs towards the indigenous community was extremely hostile and dominating and they had no respect for or mutual understanding of the original habitants of the village. They did not mix with them apart from hiring them for cheap labour such as tending their crops, looking after their animals and doing other labouring work for which they were paid meagre wages.

Both the communities - Jat Sikhs and Untouchables - were living apart from each other, not mixing socially and treating the others like aliens. The village was (and still is) separated into two similar to thousands of others all over India. There was a clear line through the middle of the village, marked by dusty tracks dividing Jat Sikhs living to the north and the Untouchables on the south side of the village. The Untouchables' side of the village was surrounded by large ponds full of dirty water, providing a safe haven for breeding mosquitoes, and mounds of smelly cow dung. The whole situation and the general environment was a ready-

9

made recipe for many diseases for those who had no means to seek proper medical treatment. The other side of the village where the Jat inhabitants were was plain level ground and less dirty compared with the other side. There were no direct road links to any main city or town and the only links to other neighbouring villages were muddy, dusty and overgrown tracks. The access to public transport such as bus or rail was available only at a distance of around three miles. The village had no shop, school, medical provision or other facilities required for daily life and modern conveniences like electricity, television and telephone could only be dreamed about.

It would be an injustice to portray just negativity about the village, as there were many positive and good things worth mentioning as well. The most beautiful things about the village were that it was surrounded by green crofts and fields of natural greenery. The sky was blue most of the time every day with plenty of sunshine, free from industrial and traffic pollution as there were no cars or large chimneys puffing dark smoke into the atmosphere, although sometimes there was some noise and pollution from fighter jets taking trial flights from a nearby military air base. During the monsoon season, however, noise pollution from an army of grouching frogs and many unknown creatures all day and night used to be extremely irritating and the heat and unbearable humidity was most uncomfortable.

The circumstances and conditions in which I was born and brought up may look strange to the Western world but are not unique to the millions of children born and brought up in this kind of environment in India. I was the second of ten children, six brothers and four sisters, and obviously it was extremely difficult for any parents to bring up such a large family particularly with a

My father, Mr Jagat Ram Bains

very limited income. My father, Mr Jagat Ram Bains, is now nearly 100 years old, a retired landless farmer and a very muscular hard working and determined man. My mother, Mrs Partapi Bains was one of the best caring and hard working mothers in the whole world. My father is extremely dedicated to his family and work and will still do anything to fulfil any need of the family. Whether it is in the burning heat of the sun or during the frosty nights of winter nothing can stop him spending long hours in the fields looking after his crops and animals. There seems to be no end to his hard work.

I cannot remember much of my childhood apart from some vague memories of playing with other children on dusty waste-land around the village. Like the other children of the village I used to help the family, doing small jobs such as taking animals for grazing and feeding them, and providing a helping hand doing some agriculture work. There used to be flooding all over the place during rainy season and we used to enjoy running round in rain and swimming in the village ponds. The most enjoyable thing, though, used to be running around miles in green crops with out any fear or frustrations and playing hide and seek.

My mother, the late Mrs. Partapi Bains who was lost to cancer in 1984.

A few months before the declaration of the independence of India in 1947 when I was about six years old, fighting between two different Muslim groups broke out in our village. I remember that I was standing in a corner, behind a small wall, looking at people fighting with spears, sticks and swords. They were lashing at each other indiscriminately, wounding and killing each other. Three persons were hacked to death on the spot and many were badly injured. Somebody came from behind, quickly picked me up and took me away from scene of the fighting. It was a horrible incident to watch particularly for child of my age, and one which I will never forget.

I can also remember the most historic moment in Indian history, the declaration of Independence on 15th August 1947 and the partition of India into India and Pakistan. It was not only the splitting of a country into two but also a bitter division of people. During the partition, the Muslim community moved out to go to Pakistan whilst Hindu and Sikh communities came over from what was to become Pakistan into India. .

Over many years I heard stories of rivalries and animosity amongst Hindus, Muslims, Sikhs and other religions that led to the killing of each other during the process of partition. An estimated one million people lost their lives in barbaric riots during the process of people moving across the new border. The Muslims from our village moved out and went across to Pakistan and their place taken over by Jat Sikh community from Pakistan. They took over everything - agricultural land, houses and rest of the property left behind by Muslims. In the beginning, they were extremely hostile to the indigenous people of the village, looking down upon and treated them like slaves.

13

PRIMARY AND SECONDARY EDUCATION

India had just became independent in 1947 and at that time education was not legally compulsory and therefore not every child was required to go to school. I started my primary school education at the age of seven. My parents decided to send me to a school at Mansoorpur Badala approximately four miles away from our village. One of my uncles, Faqir Chand, was a teacher at this school for 29 years. There was no direct road or transport link to this village apart from muddy, dusty tracks and overgrown weeds and you had to trample over them from one side to other to find level ground to walk on even in good weather. My uncle used to walk to and from school every day and I had to follow him, walking quickly but always struggling to catch him.

The school had broken boundary walls and a big tree in the middle, which was useful protection from the burning sun in summer and sometime shelter from rain. The school building itself was an old derelict and dilapidated building. There were two class-rooms whose roof had caved in many years ago and never renewed or repaired. We used to rush to a nearby farmhouse for shelter whenever it rained or during bad weather. We used to sit on dusty floor, as there were no chairs or desks in the school for the pupils and I can remember that there was only one very old chair for the headmaster and the two teachers used to sit on a low wall around the tree in the middle.

I finished my primary school education in 1953 and joined S.D. High School in Shamchurasi. This school was at a distance of about four or five miles from our village and again there was no transport between our village and the school. My parents were not in a position to afford to buy me a pedal bike and along with some other friends I used to walk to school every day.

Caste and religious prejudice was widespread not only in schools but also in every walk of life in those days and to a certain degree an acceptable normal practice. I endured some incidents of caste prejudice and personal humiliation at school. The high school was a Hindu school where 99 percent of the teachers were Hindus. Some of them were extremely fanatical, orthodox and openly hated children belonging to lower castes.

In India child punishment such as beating, slapping or smacking by teachers was very common and acceptable in school. In fact, some teachers were well known for using a stick rather than slapping or smacking a child, as they were mindful of touching children from lower castes. There used to be a custom that the children of the 9th grade gave a party to the out-going 10th grade students and all the school teachers. There were some teachers, however, who would not join any such party as all the school children would help in preparing and serving the food.

I can remember once that the school children organised a strike against caste prejudice by some teachers and that lasted for three months. After I passed my higher secondary education (matriculation), the headmaster of the school would not give me a character certificate, which I needed to undertake further education, because I was one of those children who had organised the strike. He charged me one hundred rupees to provide a character certificate which he said is a fine for organising the strike.

However, in spite of all this I thoroughly enjoyed my

secondary school education and I passed my matriculation exams with a convincing first division. My parents and the rest of the family were extremely happy with my educational achievements and it was a matter of pride for the village as I was the third child so far who had reached this level of education.

FURTHER EDUCATION

I passed my secondary education with flying colours in April 1959 and my family, friends and relatives were extremely pleased with my achievements so far. And now it was a turning point in my life to decide and choose between looking for employment or going on to further education. It was not an easy decision for me as the family was not well off financially and it was impossible for me to proceed for further education without the help and support of my family. My parents, enthusiastically encouraged by my educational achievements so far, were very much in favour of me going on to further education but some of the family members wanted me to look for some employment. There were several opportunities to join the Civil Service but I was looking for something better. In the end, encouraged by support from family, I decide to go for further education and joined S.D.College, Hoshiarpur.

This college was about twenty miles away from my village and daily travel to and from the college was a mammoth task which undoubtedly affected my concentration on education. The nearest bus or railway station was three miles from my village and to reach the railway station was extremely difficult and unpleasant particularly on cold frosty winter mornings and during the rainy season which meant walking along flooded and muddy trails and tracks. During the rainy season, in heavy rain, I used to carry an umbrella in one hand, a pair of shoes in the other, books under one arm and pair of trousers on my shoulder. I had to reach the railway station a few minutes early in order to wash my feet, put my trousers on and get ready to catch the train on time. It was a 15 mile journey by train and I still had to walk a couple of miles to the

17

college through the narrow streets of an urban city and heavy traffic, surrounded by the deafening noise of blowing horns but nothing could stop me reaching college on time. I had to walk quickly, sometimes running, breathing smoke pollution into my lungs, hiking through heavy traffic to reach college in time. Travelling used to be an extremely boring, tiring, time consuming and unpleasant experience. Adding to the misery of the walking were the ear-deafening horns, hooters and whistles of buses, lorries, scooters, trucks and all kind of vehicles, the noise of which I can still feel ringing in my ears even after fifty years.

The general environment surrounding the college was not very congenial for further education establishment - and the college was not an ideal educational institution. It comprised a dilapidated sub-standard building with black and mouldy walls, no sign of a touch of paint for many years and the smell of damp everywhere. It was situated between an extremely congested shopping area on one side and a narrow main road on the other side, full of traffic pollution and the deafening noise of the horns of passing vehicles and filthy roads full of cow dung and garbage. The college lacked basic facilities such as proper library, play-ground and other support facilities for students and we used to go around to other colleges and schools for these facilities. It was a college for the less well off and catered for students from poor backgrounds coming from far away rural villages, the majority of them on pedal cycles.

On return from the college each day, there were a million jobs waiting for me at home - tasks such as helping the family with agricultural work, and feeding and looking after the animals and so on. There was no time at all for any hobby, playing or even mixing with other youngsters in the village. I used to study for long hours at night doing my homework and revising for my college lessons. There was no electricity in those days and I had to use a paraffin lamp at night-time. It used to be extremely uncomfortable during hot and humid nights in summer, with the added discomfort and misery of an army of insects and mosquitoes flocking around the paraffin lamp. The humidity and mosquito bites often turned the rest of night into an unbelievable nightmare and some time I ended up with no sleep throughout the whole night. It was extremely difficult to concentrate on studying in these circumstances.

Life used to be totally different during the long three month summer break. There used to be a total transformation of my life from a college student to a full time farmer, helping the family doing all kinds of work, usually in dirty clothes with dusty shoes and completely unrecognisable from my normal college appearance. It used to be long hours and extremely hard work compared with western-style holidays involving eating, drinking and relaxing in order to recoup your energy. The psychological strain of thinking like a student - including homework, revision and textbooks - was completely set aside during holiday period.

While still at college I had numerous opportunities to take up government posts in the Civil Service, Army or Police Department but my parents insisted upon me completing my degree first before starting to look for employment. I was selected for a commission as Second Lieutenant in the Indian Army during the Indo-China War in 1962 in which India suffered heavy fatalities and lost Tibet to China. My parents came to know about this at the last minute from a letter inviting me for medical, which they kept hiding from me until the date had passed. Thereafter my parents had a serious discussion with me, and strictly advised against taking such decisions on my own. I exchanged correspondence with a couple of universities in England and had a very positive response.

We were encouraged to pursue our application for admission even through at the back of our minds had some concerns about financial support. The whole admission process was a bit of complicated and the procedure was lengthened as it took at least two weeks for the post to reach us. During this period, we came to know that the British government was looking for workers in various trades from India and issuing some kind of employment vouchers. This option appeared to be easy, simple and less expensive. We decided to go to England on an employment voucher and then pursue our ambition for further education once we had arrived. Three of us applied to the British embassy in New Delhi for an employment voucher and within a few weeks the documentation had arrived. Two of us took it to a travel agent who organized everything, from getting the passport to booking our air flights to the UK. My family was not happy about my decision to go abroad as no one so far from the neighbourhood had been abroad. However, eventually after some discussions within the family, they reluctantly agreed to support me.

There was a great excitement when I passed my degree in 1963, as I was the first person from the whole village who had attained such a high accolade. My parents and the rest of the family were naturally very proud of my achievement and they had high hopes and were very optimistic of my future prospects. I was very pleased with the way that everything was progressing and I was getting ready to go abroad. My parents were quick to arrange my marriage with a girl name Ram Piari a few miles away from my village before my departure. Most importantly to me, however, I was very proud of my passport which shows that in those days I had a full head of hair and a moustache.

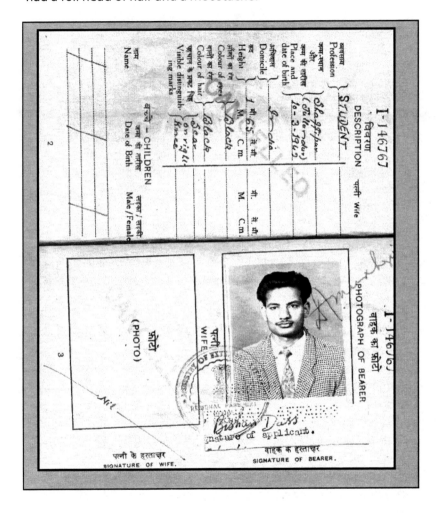

LEAVING HOME

The time had come at last for me to move on and leave my beloved village behind, the village where I was born, brought up and enjoyed playing on traffic-free but dusty roads and open fields. It was, though, a heart-breaking moment for the time was fast approaching for me to depart from my beloved parents and the rest of the family. There were more than two hundred people - including my family, friends, relatives and some from our village - who came to wish me good luck. It was a nice bright afternoon on 25th November 1963 that I made a swift move towards the local railway station about two miles away from my village. Everybody was hugging me again and again and shaking hands with me. There was an atmosphere of sadness and a sombre mood all around. I looked at their grim faces, some of them with tears in their eyes, and with lips tight closed saying a lot without having to open their mouths. I looked around time and time again, gazed at the faces of everybody, and pondered over the forthcoming separation which would be for a long unknown period.

Some of my friends and relatives came with presents and garlands made of fresh flowers to put around my neck. But now the time had come to make a move. I started out of my house and walking towards the local railway station. I looked around with my wide eyes at the grim faces some of them full of tears. I looked around repeatedly at the dusty roads, the big trees, the animals on the side of footpath and the green fields surrounding my small village. I felt depressed and sad thinking how long will it be before I see them again—or indeed, am I ever going to look upon them ever again?

FROM BOMBAY TO LONDON

I boarded the Swiss Air flight from Santa Cruz Airport in Bombay early in the morning on 29th November 1963 and started the long journey to an unknown land thousands miles away from home sweet home. It was the first time I had experienced travelling so far by air. It was the most frightening experience of my life and after another long ten-hour journey, the plane landed at Heathrow Airport at about 5.30pm.

I picked up my luggage and walked through immigration and customs without any hitch. I came out of the airport building and started looking around eagerly to see if anybody had come to meet me. But it did not took me long to face disappointment.

Now I had a most difficult question to answer, where to go from here as I had no relative or friend to whom I could go? The only contact I had was an address of a distant relative whom I had never met and was living in Wolverhampton. Scared and worried I came out of the airport and looked around for someone who may have come to help me. It was an extremely frightening and worrying situation and a real test for me to face reality thousands miles away from my homeland. I searched my pockets and eventually found the address of my relative living in the Black Country although I had no idea how far it was from London. There were taxi drivers plying for fares outside the airport and they were quick to pick on people like me who were clearly innocent and naive new-comers.

An unofficial taxi driver was quick to pick up six of us who were all in the same situation. He bundled us into his saloon car and started on a long journey on a cold, dark rainy evening, dropping us one by one in different towns and cities. I was the last one to be dropped off and we arrived in Wolverhampton at about 9.30pm. The driver knocked at the door of a dimly lit terrace house in Lesley Road in the Heath Town area of Wolverhampton. A short woman about four feet tall opened the door and reluctantly peeped outside. The taxi driver said madam you have a visitor from India. She was taken aback, looked at the man standing in front of her, *"What?"* she said, *"A visitor - your relative from India"* he replied. I slid down the window of the car and saw a small woman looking confused and shaky. I got out of the car with my bag hanging off my shoulder and looked at the woman saying *"Namaste Bhabi ji"* (Greetings, sister-in-law). She looked up at me, still speechless. I slid into the house quietly and the taxi driver carried my suitcase inside. From the outset, it looked nothing short of forced entry into someone's house.

The driver asked for his taxi fare but she said she had no money and asked him either to wait or come back later on when her husband would be back from work. He agreed to come back but on his return there were some argument about the fare as he asked for the full fare from London to Wolverhampton. My relative refused to pay the full amount as I told them that I was not alone in the taxi from London to Wolverhampton and that as he dropped the other passengers at their various destinations he had charged them full fare. In the end after some argument, a fare was agreed and the driver left.

After the taxi driver had left, the landlord shut the front door and we moved in to the living room where the inhabitants looked at me with weary eyes and sealed lips for a while. It was clear from their faces that perhaps thinking, what we are going to do with this stranger in our house, talking to each other in silence. Then, in an ice-breaking voice, NCD asked " *How are you, you had a nice journey?".* *"Yes bhaji, (brother)"* I replied in a scared voice.

Now I had the extremely difficult task of making myself acceptable and settled in a strange and totally different environment. It was not an easy task to leave a loving family behind thousands of miles away and seeking refuge amongst strangers in a foreign land. It was a family of husband and wife, two young sons and a third one on the way in just a few weeks time. The first and foremost thing was an introduction to each other and with some scary eyes as I mentioned my name the two children started mocking me, giggling and giving me a look that suggested that an alien had just landed in their house. As it was getting late now and the man had to go to work next morning. I was offered some food but I was not feeling hungry at all. Being sensitive about not upsetting them, however, I tried to force myself to eat a couple of chapattis in order to please them.

I had no sleep at all the whole night as I kept pondering over a million things which occupied my mind, thinking over again and again about my village, friends and relatives and sweet memories of the family that I had left behind, making me homesick and depressed. I got up early in the morning to face another day of hope and despair in my life. I sat on the bed for a long time just thinking about going downstairs. I was reluctant to go down, as I was not sure about the reaction of the landlord of the house. I was worried about how they would treat me, as I was an unexpected guest and a stranger into their house. At last, I took courage, slowly crept down the stairs, extremely mindful of making any noise on the creaking stairs. There was absolute silence throughout the house and I felt more than a little scared. I felt like an intruder trying to break in to someone's house.

It was, cold, dark and dull compared with the sunny and bright morning that I had left back in India. I looked all around the dining room— an old dining table and some chairs, patterned wall-paper and badly worn floor covering were all new to me. I stood by the table thinking about my next move; my tooth brush was in my bag left in the bedroom upstairs but I decided not to go back to get it as I may disturb somebody. An idea came to my mind to go into the kitchen and make a cup of tea. However, where is the kitchen? I had no idea. I walked forward and reluctantly opened a door and realised that it was indeed the kitchen. This is the first time I had the chance to look at a kitchen with worktop, tall free-standing cooker and sink. I had no idea about how to light or use the cooker, and make a cup of tea. I looked at the buttons of the gas cooker and nearby matchbox and, reluctantly, I turned the cooker on and lit it with the matches. I boiled some water in a pan, found some tea, milk and sugar, and eventually managed to make a cup of tea.

While I was sitting in the dining room sipping my drink, I heard some whisperings and voices of children in the front room, which was used as a bedroom. I reluctantly knocked on the door slightly opening it and said good morning all and had a quiet reply . *"Do you want a cup of tea Bhabi ji?"* I asked with a very humble voice. She replied *"Oh, yes"*. I felt slightly relieved and with a less heavy heart walked back into the kitchen and made a cup of tea for her. She asked me to have a seat on the chair so that we could get acquainted as I arrived late last night and there had not been enough time to introduce each other. We had a lengthy talk about my family background and she talked about her family both here and back in India. Her husband returned from work in the evening and we had meal together and talked further. There-after I felt quite relaxed and relieved of some of the pressure of being stranger in a house of strangers.

I settled down gradually within few days, mixing with the family, and adapting to new living environment and of course, the cold weather. I started doing some household work such as clean-ing, cooking, and washing, mopping, shopping and looking after small children and soon, I became a popular member of the family especially with the two young children who started calling me uncle.

After few days, Mr NDC took me to the local employment office to get me registered for a job and I started getting unemployment benefit of three pounds and fifteen shillings per week. This sum may look a small amount these days but then it was a reasonable enough to live on for one week. It was a great help in those days, and it helped me to pay the rent whilst the rest went towards food.

I used to stay inside most of the time and I had little outside contact with anybody else. Although it was wintertime and not very pleasant to go out, I often used to pop into the garden. One of the neighbours, a frail elderly woman, sometimes came out into her garden and it was clear that, lonely like myself, she was look-ing for some one to talk to. We used to enjoy talking to each other in spite of some communication problems. After some time, though, I started feeling homesick, lonely and depressed. There were no telephone lines readily available and phone calls to India was extremely expensive. Instead, I started writing letters back home almost every week without waiting for any reply for the previous one. Every letter had almost the same story involving homesickness, loneliness, cold and dull weather and being used by the people like a house servant.

RENDEZVOUS WITH LIFE

I felt very depressed, homesick, lonely and cut off from the rest of world for several months as there was no-one with whom I could share my feelings. I felt like my brain had stopped thinking and my mind was occupied for most of the time pondering over the circumstances in which I found myself. During daytime, I tried to keep myself busy doing household work, but I could hardly sleep at night. I thought about returning to India but I had no money to pay for a return ticket to my homeland, and found myself helplessly trapped here in England. I felt extremely depressed, lonely, and went through this agony every day of my life for at least three months before I concluded that there was no easy escape from the reality of life. I had no money to go back to India and it would be a disaster as I have no means of returning the money that I had borrowed to come to England originally. I decided that I had to find employment rather than going back to India.

It was not easy to talk to Mr NDC, he was a man who kept his own counsel, and I had no outside contact that could help me in finding a job. An elderly man, one of their relatives, came to the house one evening and I plucked up the courage to talk to him, asking him if he could help me to find a job. He agreed to take me around to some factories and accompany me to see a man, Mr. RL, who was a charge hand at Qualcast. We went to a pub to talk to him and he agreed to see me at the factory gates the following morning. It was the first time that I had been out looking for a job and it seemed that I had immediately struck lucky.

I got up early in the morning, walked from Lesley Road to

the Qualcast factory on Willenhall Road, and as I reached there I saw about half a dozen fellow Indians already standing by the gate looking for employment. I too stood on one side, at some distance from them, eagerly waiting Mr RL to come out and take me inside. As I was sitting on a small wall on one side, I was amused to see a funny drama taking place in front of me. I watched as other Indians repeatedly approached the manager's office, knocking on the office window and reluctantly speaking in frightened voice, asking "*Job please*". The manager opened the office window and shouted at them telling them "*Bhag jao (go way)"* in Indian. They were scared and retreated a few yards before starting again to move close to the manager's cabin, again tapping on the door and further upsetting the manager. I witnessed the incident repeated several times in front of my eyes.

The manager became even more angry and fed up with them and he called Mr RL to sort them out. When he did come out , though, I could not recognise him. His face and clothes were covered in black soot from the factory, he had a baseball cap covering his bald head, and he had still got pedal bike clips on his ankles. He reminded me of some of the street beggars in India. He spoke politely to the other men asking them to go away and leave the manager alone to do some office work as he had said that at present he had no jobs to offer. After they had left, he turned around and looked at me. He came close to me and said that he was sorry but that he had forgotten about me coming this morning and that as the manger had already told the others that there were no jobs he could not now ask him for me. He asked me to try again next day, but I did not give a second thought to going back to Qualcast, as the look of his appearance put me off. It made me to think what kind of job might be doing as a charge hand and surely, I have to do some thing worse than that.

The same elderly man that had come to the house before returned one evening and volunteered to help with taking me around to factories looking for a job. Next day we went around to a few factory gates in the Bilston area and after walking around for most of the morning, we ended up at the gate of Stewarts & Lloyds' Bilston Steel Works where, following a brief English reading test, I was offered a job of a labourer in the Labour Pool department. The following day I went to work and reported at the appointed place where there were some 10 or 12 people, all except two being Asians. We were given safety helmets and taken on a comprehensive tour of the factory. It was the first time that I had seen such a huge factory, complete with seven large furnaces and sky-high chimneys puffing thick dark smoke into the environment both day and night. I saw a wonderful massive blast furnace producing quality steel from iron ore imported from India whilst finding the noise of the heavy machinery and overhead cranes deafening. I was amazed at the intense heat from the furnaces and the dust clouds that seemed to hang in the air all over the place. It was all new to me. After the daylong tour of the factory we ended up in an office suite where we were treated to a cup of tea and biscuits before being shown a film about the practical working of the factory. At the end of the first day we were - without any doubt - under the impression that we were going to be appointed to executive type jobs. We finished the first day at about 4.30 pm and at the end of the day, we were introduced to Mr RS, an Indian person in charge of labour pool workers, and told to report to him the next day.

I started out early in the morning the following day as I did not know the proper bus route from Wolverhampton to Bilston. I had to ask several people to make sure that I caught the right bus and got off at the right bus stop. In the end I reached Bilston town centre and from there I walked to the work place at Stewarts & Lloyds on Millfields Road. I reported to the correct place and met some of the other guys who, like me, had started on the same day. Mr RS told us to pick up some tools - shovels, picks and wheel-barrows - although some of us were not very familiar with names and kept looking at each other. He suddenly realised the problem, and picked up the tools himself and gave them to us one by one.

He asked three of us to follow him outside as he wanted us to dig some trenches where they wanted to lay down some pipes or cables. It was bad weather outside - very cold, rough and rainy - and to dig rock-solid ground with a pick without any hand gloves was extremely painful. While we were struggling with the job, Mr RL was standing under a nearby railway bridge, laughing at and taunting at us. It was an extremely memorable experience and a real test of my life, as I had never gone through this kind of hard-ship and humiliation before. After working for a few days outside we were taken back inside and given jobs sweeping up and picking up heavy metal and loading it onto trucks. After working on this job for about six months I was moved to another job, which was extremely dusty in hot and humid conditions for a 12 hour long shift, seven days a week. Although I was not happy with the conditions and the whole working environment I had no choice and I accepted the job. Gradually I settled down and accepted that I would have to do whatever job I was asked to undertake.

There were 45 men—including me— working as dismantlers under three charge hands in the melting shop. I worked there for eight years. It was a gang work, consists of 15 workers in each gang with one charge hand. . Our job was to dismantle the interior of the steel furnace and repair it. Often the job meant working at least 20 feet underground to dig molten slag, sweep chimney tunnels, and pull out the waste in buckets using pulleys. It was exceptionally hard work in hot conditions and often we would be covered in chemical soot which was certainly dangerous to our health. All the workers were Indians, but the foreman and the three charge hands were all white. They were all old (in their late fifties) and unfit to do other work. It was obvious that they had no experience working on the job, and that their only qualification was that they had white skin. Our charge hand was named Chappi but everybody called him Chutia (a rude name in Indian). He was a short fat man with a flat cap covering his bald head all the time and he wore a long brown loose overcoat in all weathers.

I think it is worth mentioning here the prevailing working conditions and racial prejudice openly practiced on the shopfloor of the Bilston Steel Works. The Labour Pool was where every new worker would start working but within days the white workers would be transferred to better and secure jobs. The coloured workers had to stay in Labour Pool for several months and when they were given the chance to move to a better job, they were given the hot, dirty, low paid jobs of lower grade that nobody wants to do. Surprisingly there was no secret about it as this was being carried on under an open agreement between the management and the union. The membership of the union was compulsory under an agreement between the management and the steel union with every worker required to join the union and have union subscriptions deducted from their weekly wages. However, unfortunately the union was for white workers only and the interests of black workers never became an agenda item for them. If any Black or Asian worker ever raised concerns over equality of opportunity or objected to unfair treatment their voice fell on deaf ears. I attended a union meeting once and raised certain issues concerning working conditions, and asked for an increase of the

33

hourly pay to five shillings. I was confronted with tough opposition and humiliation. I walked out of the meeting quietly. This message was passed on to the management and consequently I was put on the black list for any promotion to a better job.

In July 1971 I had a telegram from India saying my mother was seriously ill in hospital. It was a real shock and I had a sleepless night. Next day I spoke to the manager at work and showed him the telegram. He agreed (though reluctantly) to let me go to India for few weeks. On my return from India, however, I went to the factory and reported at reception to commence work next day. The girl at the reception spoke with the manager, but he refused to take me back as he was already trying to find an excuse to get rid of me simply because of my involvement in the trade union. He told the receptionist that he had no job for the time being, although in fact I know that he took on two additional workers very shortly afterwards.

I was unemployed for about six weeks before I managed to find a job as an overhead crane driver at the Wednesbury Tube Company also in Bilston. I worked there for five or six years from 1972 to 1978 and during this period I was appointed shop steward for the Transport & General Workers Union representing some 80 or 90 shopfloor workers. .

In May 1975 I was elected to the Council of the Metropolitan Borough of Wolverhampton. I was still working for the Wednes-bury Tube Company but the management agreed to allow me time off for civic duties in line with agreement with the union. I applied for a charge hand job in 1978 and during the interview; the directors asked me a question concerning my civic duties. He said under present arrangements when you go away to meetings we

Returning from India for the first time in 1971 when my mother was ill.

normally find someone to cover your job driving of a crane but as a charge hand you would be responsible for at least 80-90 workers and who will be responsible to look after them when you have to go away for council meetings? It was a difficult question for anybody to answer and obviously it was clear that the company would not consider me for the job.

While I was at Wednesbury Tube Company, I started applying for white-collar jobs. I made several applications for various jobs but had a little success as my qualifications were from an Indian university. However, I never gave up, and eventually in 1978 I had an invitation for an interview for a job with Leicester Council for Community Relations. The interview went well and I was duly appointed as an Assistant Community Relations Officer on a three year contract. The city of Leicester was a strange place to me as I did not know anyone there. It is more than 70 miles from Wolverhampton and it would be extremely difficult to travel to work every day, particularly in a bad weather. Therefore, I had to stay there for five nights a week.

On the first day I travelled to work in my car with a suitcase and other utility things in car boot. I had an introductory meeting with my senior colleague and other staff members. After I settled down in my office I asked Raj (to whom I reported) to help me find lodgings. He said that was no problem as his aunt had a spare room. During lunchtime we went around to her house. She had her married son and a grandson living with her and Raj introduced me to them, speaking very highly about me telling them that I was highly qualified and just appointed as his assistant.

They were pleased to take me as lodger and showed me around their house. We had a pleasant chat over a nice cup of tea together. While we were sitting in the lounge talking, his aunt asked politely in her very low voice about my caste. I was shocked and I pretended that I did not hear her. She repeated her question and with a little smile I replied that Raj has already told you about me. It was clear that was not enough for her, and she was determined to learn about my roots. She asked again about my background in India. *"I am a human being here and was the same back in India"* I replied politely. I could see deep-rooted caste prejudice behind her smile. I felt uneasy and wanted to get out of her house as soon as possible. We returned to the office but I told Raj nothing about his aunt. It seemed that I would have to continue commuting back home each evening until I found some suitable accommodation. Eventually I made contact with a local man who was able to offer me more suitable lodgings.

At the end of my three year contract I took a job as an Estate Officer with Walsall Council's Housing Department. I was put in charge of Goscote, one of the most deprived housing estates in the borough. I worked on this job for a year and became very popular amongst local residents. Then the local authority restructured the management of the estate eliminating my job. The new management system was introduced without any consultation with my union or with me and under those circum-stances I felt I had to invoke the grievance procedure and seek the support of my union. Then, following negotiations the Council reviewed my case and signed an agreement that in future it would not repeat this situation or move me to another office without prior consultation. The Goscote residents and tenants organisa-tion (which was led by an independent member of the Council) took a deputation to see the director to try to keep me there. I was extremely surprised at this as others in my job before me never had this kind of support and trust shown by the people of this estate.

I worked seven years at Bentley Neighbourhood Office as an Assistant Neighbourhood Officer. During this time I had several opportunities to take over the manager's job but I always avoided such a temptation as being an assistant I had fewer responsibilities and more freedom to go about my civic duties as a member of Wolverhampton Council. After working for seven years in this role, some of my colleagues and senior officers of the housing department persuaded me to apply for the Neighbourhood Officer position. Now it was Tory controlled authority with the majority councillors on the interview panel being from the controlling group. Obviously they knew that I was a Labour councillor with the neighbouring authority and I was not surprised when I was not successful in my application. They appointed a junior person to the job who was a receptionist at my office and who also happened to be the son of a councillor. At this I resigned instantly as I found this discriminatory and insulting. Supported by the Commission for Racial Equality I took the Council to an Industrial Tribunal but ultimately lost the case as the law did not cover political discrimination. After this, I set up my own retail business, which I ran for ten years.

COMMUNITY ACTIVITIES

For many years Asians living here in UK had been subject to discriminatory treatment and racial prejudice. It was extremely difficult for them to find lodgings with indigenous people and vendors often instructed estate agents not to sell their house to blacks. Racism was quite open and an acceptable norm in life. Pubs and clubs had discretion to exclude black customers and it was not unusual to see a notice on their windows saying 'Blacks and Asians are not allowed'. I had personal experience of being told by certain landlords against talking to my friends in my mother tongue Punjabi, as other customers feel offended.

They were destined to live in squalor in run-down inner city areas. I heard stories of people living in extremely over crowded conditions where as many as 20 or 30 people lived in a terraced slum house. They worked long shifts, sharing beds or old mattresses on the floor turning every room into a bedroom at night. There are many humorous stories of people having to stand in a queue for a long time waiting for their turn to use the kitchen or bathroom.

The colour and racial prejudice reached its peak during the 1960s and 70s when British society was torn apart. The majority of first generation Asians came here during this period on employment vouchers issued by the British government. Acute housing problems and unemployment contributed to deprivation and slums and forced people to live in ghettoes. This gave rise to opportunist right wing movements blaming the recently arrived coloured migrants for the shortage of housing as well as unemployment, deprivations and all the evils of society. The life and properties of Asians and Blacks were constantly under

39

threat—and then Mr Enoch Powell's 'Rivers of Blood' speech fuelled the situation, adding further to racial tension.

For a sense of security against regular racial attacks strengthened the bonds of unity amongst third world migrant communities. They felt destined to live in ghettoes, in run-down inner city areas of slum housing with a poor environment but where they felt safe and could look after their property. The racial tension often spilled over into street clashes adding further to sense of insecurity and many felt too threatened to go out alone. The period of sixties was marred with racial tension with white skinhead gangs roaming town centres at night, looking for prey, attacking any blacks that they came across. Late night shift workers such as bus drivers and conductors were regularly targeted and 'Paki bashing' was popular and a source of pleasure amongst many white youngsters. They seemed unaware of their actions which frequently resulted in psychological injuries far deeper and longer lasting than physical wounds. Many community organisations such as the Anti-Nazi League, Indian Workers Association, Inter Faith Group, Socialist Workers Organisation and Trade Union Organisations united to fight against racist elements in our society.

While I was working at the Bilston Steel Works I started taking some interest in organisations such as Anti-Nazi League, Council for Community Relations, Indian Republican Group of G.B. (an overseas organisation of the Republican Party of India) and Sh. Guru Ravidas Dharmak Sabha, Wolverhampton. I was an active member of some of these organisations for several years and held offices of assistant secretary, secretary and chairperson. I had the opportunity to meet and greet several distinguished personalities and political leaders from abroad, particularly India.

Among those I had met and organized their public functions and meetings were the Prime Minister of India, V.P. Singh, Harkishan Singh Surjit who was Secretary of CPI, the Dalai Lama, the spiritual leader of Tibet, Yashvant Rao Ambedkar, the son of Dr.B.R.Ambedkar, Lahori Ram Bali Leader of RPI India, Nanak Chand Rattu PA of Dr.B.R.Ambedkar and many more.

Welcoming Yashvant Rao Ambedkar at Heathrow Airport on his first visit to UK. In the photo, I am on his right, behind me is Kushi Ram Jhumat, and on the right Mr Gamerey and Rattan Lal Sampla.

The first generation of Indians, although thousands miles away from their motherland, were very close to the political and social life of India. There were not many Indian newspapers available in this country but even then I used to get hold of a weekly, called *The Blitz* and *Bheem Patrika* by post from India. People were keen to take an active part in discussions about Indian political and social changes. There were some pubs well known for lively discussion involving issues of mutual interest such as Indian politics, religious, social and community matters. Often discussion and arguments fuelled by alcohol used to become more interesting and tense. People from ethnic minorities, in particular from the Asian sub-continent were settling down gradually, finding jobs, buying their own houses, sorting out a family and social life. Most of the elder generation were, by tradition, law-abiding, hard working people.

There were some Asian organisations who held annual conferences and functions at the Civic Hall and Wulfrun Hall in Wolverhampton at which people discussed and talked about political and social life as well as exploitation and poverty back in India. In 1968, the Shankracharia of Puri made a public statement confirming and endorsing Untouchability as right according to the Hindu religion. There was a huge uproar throughout the whole world condemning his statement and demanding that the Indian government should prosecute him for inciting caste and racial hatred in India. The Indian Republican Group of Great Britain, of which I was secretary, organised a demonstration against the Shankraharia of Puri in London. It was a most memorable protest as it was the first time such a large demonstration took place outside India. There were more than 7,000 people who, having gathered at Hyde Park, then marched through the streets of London, and presented a memorandum to the High Commissioner of India urging the then current Indian government to prosecute Shankracharia of Puri.

Some of these organisations were lacking clear direction, a proper agenda and manifesto. I realised that I was wasting my time as these organisations were not doing anything constructive to promote the interests of those they claimed to represent. They

The London protest against the Shankracharia of Puri. I am standing on the front of the banner on my right is Dalip Chand Nahar, Kirpa Ram Jassa, and Khushi Ram Jhumat. On the far right in the crowd is Mehar Chand Jassal.

were wasting a great deal of time arguing amongst themselves, fighting for positions and offices within their organisations. I decided to distance myself from them in order to better concentrate on looking after my family and work.

LOCAL POLITICS

It was during that time that I came across some of local Labour Party workers such as Alan Garner, John Bird and Mordecai James. We met at a function at the Civic Hall and, after the function was over, we had a chance to speak to each other and we realised that there was a great deal of common ground between us. Alan Garner lived in Begot Street, not far from my house in Napier Road, and he became a close friend and started coming to my house (particularly during election times) asking for my help and support to deliver leaflets.

He asked me few times to join the Labour Party but I was not too keen to get involved to that extent, simply due to the fact that I was working 12 hours a day, six days a week and I was thinking of enrolling at a college for further education. Alan regularly approached me over the next two years and eventually persuaded me to join the party. I joined the Labour Party in 1968 with a view to providing help and support to the party off and on and particularly during the elections. However, Alan started taking a keen interest in me and he wanted to promote me to become an elected member of the council. He managed to get me appointed to two school governing bodies and we worked closely for local and national elections for several years.

There was a local government boundary change during the year of 1973 and the Labour Party was looking for quite a few new candidates to stand in the May council elections. I was put on the list of would-be candidates without any interview and eventually short-listed for the Blakenhall ward, traditionally a Tory stronghold in those days. I spoke to Alan Garner and discussed in detail my circumstances concerning my family and availability of time from work. I understood that it was a big commitment and I was not ready as yet for it as I had my other priorities in life. However, Alan thought that I was just making excuses, and was determined to push me to become candidate the following year.

There was a selection meeting a week after the short listing and it was my intention not to attend the selection meeting. Alan Garner was fully aware of my feelings and intention. He came to my house early on the day of the selection meeting and insisted upon me coming to the meeting. He was adamant that he would not leave my house until I agreed to accompany him to the Labour Party meeting. His efforts were convincing, genuine and sincere and I found it difficult to decline as I was mindful not to disappoint him and in the end I conceded that I would accompany him to the selection meeting.

The meeting of the Blakenhall Labour party was held in Sept. 1972 at the Dudley Road Primary School in order to select candidates for the council elections in 1973. I was one of three candidates selected to contest the seat. The other two candidates were Jack Haywood and John Johnson. I was perhaps the first ever ethnic-minority candidate to stand for election to the Metropolitan Borough Council of Wolverhampton—in fact very few from the ethnic minorities were even aware of their democratic rights and had little knowledge of how to exercise them. They were not very familiar with the administrative and democratic system of this country, mainly because the first generation of immigrants who came to U.K. during the early sixties had other priorities such as employment and housing in their minds. The majority of them were of the opinion that after working here for a few years they would go back to the country of their origin.

Blakenhall ward was a strong Tory-controlled ward of the Council and at the election we lost (although not unexpectedly but by a narrow margin). This helped me gain a great deal of experience which provided a springboard for my election campaigns in the future. Whilst it was not a surprise that I did not win the election my campaign certainly stimulated a great deal of excitement and interest amongst people from the ethnic minority community. Subsequently many people from this group were encouraged to take part in mainstream community organisations and political activities as well as becoming more aware of their rights here in this country. There were many who were surprised to know that coloured people from an ethnic minority could stand as candidates and take part in the democratic system of the United Kingdom. What is more, the majority of them were illiterate, unable to read or write English. They were dependent upon others to interpret and fill in all sorts of complicated forms. I was one of several who used to volunteer to help them wherever possible.

The Labour Party was very pleased with the 1973 election results and I became well known within the local party. The Party was very supportive and they were looking for a safe seat for me when in 1975, a vacancy arose suddenly in St. Peter's ward. Councillor Shadi Sharma who had been elected to the council in 1973 resigned his seat. He was a brilliant, rising star and hard-working young man but he was not readily acceptable to some who believed that monopolising the leadership of certain ethnic groups was their hereditary right. Councillor Shadi Sharma was forced to resign as he was made a scapegoat after false allegations, smear propaganda and victimisation by the Indian Workers Association were made against him.

47

My first election leaflet from the 1973 campaign.

BLAKENHALL WARD

Blakenhall is begining to look brighter, with the tidying of the Dudley Road and the work, which is shortly to begin on extending Blakenhall Gardens Shopping Centre. Work has begun on Colton Hills School, which will provide a good education for all our secondary school children in very pleasant surroundings, and a new nursery school has been built in Phoenix Street. A room has been set aside for community purposes in Dudley Road School. The old rubbish tip between Dudley Road and Thompson Avenue is being tidied and will soon be in use for recreational purposes.

We have helped to continue the work of making this a more pleasant area to live in by electing Sam Reynolds to represent us on the West Midlands Council; let us now take this a stage further by voting, as electors of Blakenhall Ward, for three Labour Candidates and for a Labour Council in Wolverhampton. You will receive an official poll card from the Town Hall. Please take it with you when you go to the polling station on Thursday, 10th May, 1973 to vote for

BISHAN DASS	X
JACK HACKWOOD	X
GEORGE JOHNSON	X

your Labour Party Candidates

Published by G. Howells, 4 Welgwood Close, Wolverhampton.
Printed by The Birches Printers, Croft Street, Walsall.

Once again you, the voters in Blakenhall, have a decision to make. You have to decide whether you want councillors who will represent you and who understand the problems you face, regarding education, social services and the community, housing, traffic, and so on - problems both with the ward and which face Wolverhampton as a whole. We, your Labour candidates, are aware of your problems because we are in touch with people in the ward and in the rest of Wolverhampton, and we feel that we have the ability and the conscience to work for you on the Council and in its Committees.

*   *   *

We ask for your support at the Council Election on Thursday, 10th May, 1973. The decision on who represents you is entirely in your hands.

BISHAN DASS

JACK HACKWOOD

GEORGE JOHNSON

BISHAN DASS — Married with two children. Wolverhampton resident 10 years; active member of Blakenhall Labour Party. Keenly interested in social welfare, racial harmony and community relations. Graduate of Punjab (India) University. Plays leading role in Indian Republican Group of Great Britain.

JOHN HACKWOOD — Member A.U.E.W. Branch referee; Branch Trustee; Provisional Delegate, District Committee Member, Blakenhall Labour Party; Vice Chairman, South East Wolverhampton West Midlands Member, West Midlands Labour Party Local Government Committee; Executive member and Trades Union Liaison Officer; Wolverhampton Central Labour Party.

GEORGE JOHNSON — Married with three children. In Grenadier Guards ten years. In Member Transport and General Workers' Union District Committee; Delegate to Wolverhampton & Bilston District Trades Council and member of Executive Committee. On various local Committees.

I shared this with two other candidates, John Hackwood and George Johnson.

The St. Peter's ward Labour Party invited me for interview and I was subsequently selected to contest the seat. The other two ward councillors, Mordecai James and Ian Claymore (my election agent) provided me with great help and support in organising the election campaign. There was a huge enthusiasm in the local Asian community as they were very encouraged to see a candidate from within their own community. I was certainly not short of volunteers to help me and I won the seat with a comfortable majority. It was not just about winning a council seat but the beginning of a new era in the history of this country. The ethnic minorities who were thinking of themselves as being aliens in this wonderland suddenly started realising that they had equal rights here. Many of them had considered themselves as temporary residents here but their thinking started changing gradually and they began considering their future in this country. Indeed, some of them were encouraged to join mainstream community organisations and political parties, thus paving the way for integration and greater community cohesion.

For the first few months, I tried to learn as much as possible about the management and working arrangements of the council and for this I had to rely upon my senior mentors. There were no provisions as such compared to these days for any induction or training for newly elected members, and everyone had to learn from your own practical experience. There was no backup services such as members support services, telephone or computer facility for elected members to deal with casework and keeping in touch with their constituents. Fortunately I had experience already in public speaking before being elected to the council, an art which I had learnt back at college in India. I know well that good public speaking is a key to a successful public life and in addition, the experience and knowledge I had working with various organisations helped me to build up my self-confidence. Various departments of the council were scattered in buildings all over the town and it was difficult to make myself known and accepted by the front line staff of the council but within a few months I became familiar with council work and had started taking part in discussions at the standing committee meetings, as well as making regular contribution at full council meetings.

There were not many elected members from ethnic minorities on councils at that time; in fact there were only three of us in the whole UK. In fact, I was the second in Wolverhampton and I was aware that the people from ethnic minorities had high expectations of me. I had people coming to me with all sort of problems such as housing, education, social services, immigration and nationality; people were thinking I was the panacea for all their problems. I was keen to provide help and support to anyone coming to me, and I always tried my best to help resolve their problems. Some of the casework was extremely complicated, such as immigration, nationality, passport and visa problems. As I was not in a position to assist and had very little experience in handling all such complicated issues, in the circumstances I used to refer some such cases to local Members of Parliament who were in most of cases very helpful. I am particularly grateful to the late Bob Edwards MP for the Wolverhampton South East constituency for his help and support in dealing with such issues and many other problems. The other local Member of Parliament Mrs Rene Short, however, was often reluctant to take any case-work from outside her constituency and often I had rows with her over her refusals to assist.

90 Napier Road,
Wolverhampton

You and only you, the residents of St. Peter's Ward, are to decide whether you want to be governed by the Tories or served by your Labour representatives in Council. For the betterment of present and coming generations you have to decide whether you want a councillor who will represent you and understand the problems you face, regarding education, housing, traffic, social welfare and other community problems.

Already you have made a sensible decision by electing Mordecai James and Ian Claymore, two Labour Councillors, who are working extremely hard to make this part of Wolverhampton more pleasant to live in.

I as your Labour Candidate am fully aware of the problems of the Ward and think that with my ability, capability and consciousness, by joining the other two councillors I can help to solve these problems. So your support for me will make your hands more strong to help yourself.

BISHAN DASS

Some of Labour's achievements in St. Peter's Ward —

* **Community and Youth centre** being built in Whitmore Reans.
* **Primary school** under construction.
* **Public phones** installed in high council flats.
* New Whitmore Branch Library.
* Excellent **shopping centre** in Whitmore Reans.
* Children's play area in Park Village.

Your Ward Labour representatives will continue to press for —
* **Better bus services** in Whitmore Reans.
* **A dog pound.**
* More **school places** — nursery, primary and secondary.
* Greater priority for a **Health Centre.**
* Improved **street lighting and footpaths.**

THURSDAY, 1ST MAY, 1975
WOLVERHAMPTON
BOROUGH COUNCIL
ELECTION
ST. PETER'S WARD

BISHAN DASS
Your LABOUR Candidate

Wolverhampton resident 12 years.
Qualified as B.A. at Punjab (India) University.
Active member of T.G.C.W.U. and Branch Officer.
Active member of Blakenhall Ward Labour Party.
Member at Wolverhampton South East Labour Party Management Committee.
Previously Labour Candidate for Blakenhall Ward.
Governor, Ward Road Primary School.
Keenly interested in social welfare, racial harmony, community relations and education.

VOTE LABOUR —

vote
D A S S | X

Published by I. Claymore, 8 Sandwell Road, Foddhouses, Wolverhampton.
Printed by The Birches Printers, Croft Street, W'hall.

My leaflet for the 1975 election at which I successfully won the St Peter's ward.

YOUR LABOUR COUNCIL WORKS FOR YOU

Left—Woden House—home for the aged

Centre—Wilkinson School, Bradley

Right—Dudley Street pedestrian precinct

A SOCIAL POLICY FOR ALL. Your Labour Council has acted with imagination and compassion to achieve considerable progress in all areas of social services. Principally since 1973, we have provided an extra 155,000 meals on wheels; sixty additional home helps, with another thirty planned this year, now serve the aged and sick. We have continued to open homes and hostels for children in care, senior citizens, the mentally ill and socially deprived.

A HOUSING POLICY FOR ALL. Labour won control of Wolverhampton in May 1973 and immediately began increasing the number of Council built homes from a derisory two hundred a year under the Tories to a planned one thousand starts in 1975. Modernisation of pre-war Council homes has been boosted, and private householders have received grants and loans amounting to half a million pounds for the purpose of improving their own homes. Ten times as many mortgages have been advanced to private house buyers by Labour compared with the last year of Tory control, and a more generous rent and rate allowance scheme now operates for widows and senior citizens—all part of your Labour Council's housing policy.

AN EDUCATION POLICY FOR ALL. Major steps forward have been taken by your Labour Council towards full comprehensive education in Wolverhampton. Ninety six per cent of all our children will be attending comprehensive schools by September 1975. Nursery education has been developed, and in the next eighteen months two thousand new places will have been created. Education of the mentally and physically disabled has been approached with the resolve to secure a responsive environment for our more unfortunate children. Training for young workers and re-training for adults has been expanded to take account of economic and industrial changes. Financial resources have been limited, but Labour's dynamic policies have improved educational opportunity for all sections of our community.

A COMMUNITY DEVELOPMENT POLICY FOR ALL. Labour will continue to encourage all aspects of cultural, leisure and sporting activities, both municipally and through voluntary organisation. The Civic Hall and Art Galleries have been developed, and the indoor bowling green at the Wulfrun Hall has been particularly well received. Labour initiated successful public participation in the planning of the Linear Park, and community life has been improved without extra expense by co-ordinating existing facilities. Labour will continue to support the Council for Community Relations in the belief that it is possible for all citizens in our society to live together.

RATES REFORM—THE LABOUR PARTY ACTS FOR ALL. Labour believes the rating system should be more buoyant and broadly based. Immediately the Labour Government was elected, it appointed an independent committee to consider changes. This year, in response to pressure from Labour Councillors, massive extra financial relief is being given to domestic ratepayers by the Labour Government.

FOR AN EVEN BETTER WOLVERHAMPTON BETTER VOTE LABOUR

My leaflet emphasised my concern over social issues.

53

PROSECUTION

I had never been in trouble with the law of the land for the entire period of my life as this is how I was brought up and educated back in India. In addition, from a very young age I adopted a very strict code of practice based upon the four golden rules of principles, honesty, integrity and moral standard which I felt were most essential for a successful public life. I strongly believe that in public life you must maintain a minimum standard of behaviour, avoid taking any financial responsibility as people will be quick to blame you for any irregularities, that you must maintain high moral standards and stick to principles that you believe in strongly. These principles had been an inspirational source of strength in my life and helped build my self-confidence.

It was a struggle to be established at the council as there were barriers and resistance to acceptance and even recognition of a member from the ethnic minorities. There was no such thing as equality of opportunity and racial prejudice was the norm of the day. I had personal experience of being treated differently from other elected members of the council. I started challenging and raising questions about equality of opportunity and the underlying racial prejudice that existed in employment and the delivery of services. I was astonished to find the gravity of the racial problem at every level and that there was a great degree of resistance from all sides including elected members and council employees. Often my stand landed me in deep water and I found myself surrounded by many enemies who were quick to criticise me instead of accepting the facts and trying to find ways and means of rectifying the problem. Soon I became a thorn in the flesh of some of my council colleagues, in particular those from the opposition party and they were looking for every possible opportunity to discredit my public reputation.

Eventually in June 1976, I gave them the opportunity they sought. I took two of my children away to India and due to some unavoidable circumstances I was unable to bring them back within the time allowed and I was accused of keeping my children away from school for a period longer than the permitted time. I had spoken to the headmaster before I left for India and he had reminded me to bring the children back in time so as to set an example for others. While we were away in India, however, my younger child became sick and the doctor advised against travelling. As a consequence I had to extend my stay for few more days until the child became fit to travel.

On my return from India I contacted the education department regarding the arrangements for school for children. I was told they had to go through a medical check up before being re-admitted to school—but that we would have to wait seven weeks for the appointment. I really could not see the logic of such a delay for medical check up. My children had been away from school for four weeks and a further seven week period for before they could return to school seemed ridiculous. I knew that it was a waste of time to argue with the lady at reception, as she did not want to understand the logic and was clearly not concerned about my children's education.

Then just four days after, we had a shocking surprise through the post. A letter from court with a double summons in my name and that of my wife for keeping children away from school for an extended period. I rushed to the Civic Centre to talk to the leader of the council, Councillor John Bird and he advised me to talk to Mr Michael Duffell, the head of Legal Services at the Council. He looked at the summons but refused to interfere or provide me with any help or advice as the case was subjudice. I considered then all the circumstances involving the issuing of the summons and came to conclusion that it was a calculated conspiracy to publicly defame and discredit me. I found out from reliable sources that never before had the council taken such drastic action against any parent.

In the circumstances, I was left with no alternative but to consult a lawyer. He advised me that the maximum fine for each conviction would be five pounds, making a total of £20 for the four convictions. I said to him that I am prepared to pay him £80 to represent my case at court in order to have our names cleared. He was surprised and asked me why I was prepared to spend £80 instead of just the £20 in fines. I then disclosed to him that I was a local councillor and told him that I wanted to pay any price to have my name cleared. I told him that I strongly believe that there is conspiracy against me and that I was sure that an opposition party councillor who was chair of a local primary school, with the collaboration of head teacher and education officers of the council, had hatched a conspiracy against me.

My wife and I reached at the court in North Street, Wolverhampton early in the morning of the day of hearing and we sat in a corner of the court. We were extremely nervous as this was the first time we seen courts like this. The case against me took a full day at the hearing and all my doubts about racial prejudice and character assassination proved positive at the court hearing. My lawyer challenged the Education Welfare Officer of the local authority undercross-examination. He asked questions about how many parents took their children abroad and how many had overstayed the permitted period during the last 12 months. He asked how many parents had they prosecuted so far for taking their children abroad, for which the education welfare officer failed to provide answers. My lawyer challenged and told him that you are more concerned about the parents, particularly a father who is a coloured person and a local councillor, than the educational welfare of the children.

At the end of the day, I was hugely relieved when the case against me was dismissed on grounds of unavoidable circumstances. I had legal costs awarded to me and, of course, the case against my wife was summarily dismissed for the same reasons. After the hearing both of us walked into the office of the *Express & Star* in Queen St., talked to a reporter, and told him the whole story. To our great surprise, though, they never printed the story although I am certain that the paper would have printed full details of the case with front-page headlines had I lost and been convicted by the court.

After the case was over I started a campaign to change the law so that others would not have to go through this kind of traumatic experience. Within a week I had moved a resolution at the Labour group meeting to change the rules to allow parents to take their children away for an extended period. There was opposition to this resolution from within the Labour group as some of members were talking about the law of the land. The resolution was approved despite this opposition and was forwarded to the Association of Metropolitan Authorities for nationwide support.

1979 LOCAL ELECTIONS

I had now settled at into my role as a councillor and I became used to my council business and establishing good relationship with many of the electors in my ward. The first few years passed smoothly but at the beginning of the fourth year circumstances started changing and took a dramatic twist by the end of year 1978.

The old Indian village politics of caste prejudice and religious hatred started creeping in to undermine my position as an elected member of the Metropolitan Borough Council of Wolverhampton. The agenda was skilfully organised by a group of people mainly from Jat Sikh community disguised in the name of the Indian Workers Association. They started a smear campaign to discredit and tarnish my public reputation, using every method such as printing and distributing leaflets, writing articles in the Asian press and writing lengthy letters to the local and national leaders and party executives of the Labour Party. They left no stone unturned to get me deselected as the next candidate for the local elections in 1979. In the end, however, their efforts proved futile and I was duly elected to the council with a comfortable majority. The votes for the 1979 election were:

Bishan Dass (Labour) 2241,
G Hodson (Conservative) 1363,
N.Noor (Independent Labour) 1220,
D.Croft (Liberal) 410,
R.Smith (Rate Payers) 189,
J.Lees (National Front) 183.

Most of the votes for Naranjan Singh Noor came from one

small part of the community and, despite the fact that he had a high public profile (he was the national President of the Indian Workers Association, a member of the Marxist party and well known Punjabi poet) but even then my detractors failed to unseat me.

The question has to be asked why they decided to contest my seat rather than any of the other 19 around the borough and it seems that it was primarily down to the fact that they felt unable to accept a candidate who belonged to a scheduled caste to be elected to the council. They had adopted the strategy and organisation of the whole election campaign exactly along the lines that elections were conducted back in India. They used divisive tactics and introducing sensitive issues to heighten the sentiments of many Indian voters in the ward. They had no election manifesto except to defeat Bishan Dass. They arranged for a large number of members of the Indian Workers Association from all over the country to descend on the streets of St. Peter's ward of Wolverhampton to preach their message.

A gang of unruly youngsters started to harass my supporters and me during the election period. They chased us all over, used abusive language and threatening behaviour against us and acted in an intimidating and uncivilised manner. Not only that but a group of children regularly damaged our cars by throwing paint and stones on them and forced me to ask extra police protection. The streets were littered with fly postings whilst my election posters on lamp-posts were ripped off or repeatedly disappeared overnight. Even the bad weather on election day did not deter my enemies going out all day in streets harassing and intimidating voters and pressurising them to vote for other candidates.

Talk of politics in pubs used to be very popular and a point of attraction in those days with very lively and interesting discussions frequently continuing well after closing time. *The Ash Tree* in Whitmore Reans and *Lucian Arms* in Park Village were two of the most popular venues with every room over-crowded especially over the weekends. Nobody would win the arguments (although in financial terms the licensee no doubt ended up making a tidy profit). A group of people wanted to talk to me on a Saturday night in *The Ash Tree* and it seems that the Indian Workers Association came to know about this arrangement. They organised to fill the pub as soon as the doors opened.

Before I was due to go to the pub a person came to my house and said that I should not go there as some of those present had knives in their pockets and he had heard them whispering, planning to stab me in the back. A second man arrived looking frightened and with the same warning. My father, who was on a visit to UK, urged me keep out of it. Then a third person knocked my door. This was Sarwan Singh, widely known by his nickname Sipahee (Indian policeman). My father told him that he was extremely worried about the situation in the pub and had advised us against going there. Sarwan said *"Uncle, any knife will have to go through my chest to reach him."* He held my wrist and said, *"Come with me brother, nobody will have the courage to touch you as long as I am with you"*. As soon as we arrived at the pub, we found scores of people both inside and outside the pub. Indeed we found it difficult to get inside as a group of them was blocking the door. Eventually we managed to squeeze into the pub but the whole situation was extremely intimidating, scary and volatile. I said to them that there would be no political meeting, if only because we do not want to jeopardise the licence of the landlord and then I walked out of the pub.

Another tactic used was to report me to the police blaming me for some election irregularities. They took a deputation to see the chief superintendent of police and to lodge a complaint against me. However, the police refused to intervene unless they make a written complaint which they refused to do.

One stunt that they tried which went horribly wrong for them   involved a young boy who attended Grove Primary School. He was persuaded to wear a brightly coloured turban to school, an action that provoked his schoolmates to ridicule and make a joke of him. The bullying and harassment caused him a great deal of distress and subsequently the headmaster decided to send the child home for his own safety. A demonstration in front of the Grove Primary School was organised by the Asian Workers Association who distributed literature labelling Mr. Ernie Roden the headteacher as a racist. He immediately took court action against Mr Noor for defamation, an action that he was to go on and win. Mr Noor was fined and ordered to pay legal costs.

The Association left no stone unturned in their efforts to defeat me but ultimately they failed badly as I not only retained the seat but did so with an increased majority. There is no doubt that the electorate showed huge confidence in me and the Labour Party for which I shall be forever grateful. I must say, however, that the whole credit goes to a group of dedicated and loyal Labour Party supporters who worked hard to ensure a Labour victory. I was pleased at the solidarity and support given by people across the board and from many different backgrounds and denominations, old, young, and black and white. I would like to thank some of those who provided unparalleled help and support were Councillor Ian Claymore, Andrew Johnson, Mr. Mohan Lal Sharma, (now chairman of Shri Krishna Mandir, Wolverhampton)

Mr. Gian Singh Kandola, Giani Resham Singh chair of IWA, GurDave Cheema, Manjit Singh Kamla (a well known poet), Tarlochan Singh Chan (a world renowned song writer) and radio presenter and poet Surinder Sager. In addition, my sincere thanks also go to Asgar Khan and Mohammed Kazi (secretary Wolverhampton Central Mosque) for keeping the large Muslim community solidly behind me.

I would also like to mention the names of three most dedicated elderly persons, Babu Ram Jassal, Rulda Ram and Kirpa Ram Jassal for their excellent help and support during the election. Unfortunately, they are no more in this world. They had suffered caste prejudice and untouchability particularly back in India. They were not well-educated but were politically well-enlightened and dedicated persons. Despite not being in good health all three kept going on and on, all day from early morning until late evening, in good or bad weather, canvassing from door to door, meeting people whilst walking on foot, meeting people in pubs, shops and roads and encouraging them to vote for me.

1983 LOCAL ELECTION

Subsequently the Indian Workers Association realised that it was difficult for them to defeat me at elections and they adopted a different strategy and tactics in order to try to dislodge me from the council seat. They started infiltrating the St. Peter's ward Labour Party by enrolling a large number of members from their organization. They paid membership fees from their own pockets and used local addresses for people living anywhere, even outside Wolverhampton. I alerted the local Labour Party but they failed to control this kind of manipulation and malpractice. By the end of 1982, they had managed to get enough members enrolled into the Labour Party to ensure my deselection at the next short-listing and selection meetings.

The selection meeting for the 1983 local election was held at the Wolverhampton Civic Centre during November 1982. On the day of the selection meeting, a large number of members of the Indian Workers Association were rushing around in cars bringing in "their" Labour Party members. They were openly seen handing over Labour Party cards to people in the Civic Centre car park and sending them in to the meeting to impersonate others they had never seen before. There were unusually a large number of members present at this selection meeting - normally there are between six and 20 members present at such meetings but for this meeting the total attendance was 107.

I was fully aware of the outcome of the meeting well in advance of the voting and I knew that I stood no chance of being selected. Consequently I was not under any pressure at all or worried about losing my seat. In my five minutes speech, in a cheerful mood, I congratulated them for their hard work and dedication to bring about so many people to the meeting. No doubt, I said, you are going to achieve what you have been trying to for some time and I reminded them that they would regret their actions for the rest of their lives. There was a direct contest between myself and Roger Lawrence, now the leader of the Council and looking for a council seat for the first time. I lost the contest by four votes after a great deal of controversy involving the eligibility of people taking part at the meeting. After the meeting was over Roger came around and apologised to me. I said to him that there is no need for you to apologise, it was not your fault. After the selection meeting I came to know from reliable sources that the Indian Workers Association and their associates had a victory celebration in a nearby pub. The *Express and Star,* the local paper, printed headlines the following day that the Labour Party had deselected Bishan Dass from St. Peter's ward.

However, unfortunately their celebrations did not last very long. Within a few days, I had an invitation for an interview from the Heath Town ward Labour Party and was selected to contest the next local election in that ward. The Indian Workers Association felt hugely humiliated and turned their sights on Mr Noor, blaming him for misleading the organisation and consequently he was stripped off all the party titles and expelled from the association. A number of other community organisations distanced themselves from him including the Communist Party which took the drastic decision of cancelling his party membership. Suddenly he found himself bewildered and isolated. He approached me a few weeks before the local elections and apologised for everything took place so far and offering his support for the next election. I must say I was not amused at all by his offer of support, in fact I was extremely surprised. I was very reluctant to accept the offer and instead advised him to liaise with the Heath Town ward Labour party and some other people already working for me. He failed to do this but instead he turned up at our campaign office on the election day. He soon realised that his presence was not welcome and left the office quietly. I won the Heath Town seat with a comfortable majority, ensuring another four years membership of the Council.

MAYOR ELECT NOMINATION

Mr Ken Purchase, an ex-Member of Parliament, was my fellow councillor for the Heath Town ward and we both used to work for Walsall council in the Housing Department (although based at different site offices). He came to my office one day in November 1983 just before closing time and said that he had come to talk to me about nominations for the mayoralty for the following year. He said that he wanted to propose my name at the next group meeting. I said to him that I am not ready for it yet, and I had never even thought about becoming the Mayor. I could not, therefore, agree with his proposal and tried my best to persuade him to not to propose my name. He told me that some of the Labour members of the council had decided already to put my name forward and so he proposed my name at a group meeting in November 1983. When it came to the vote, however, I lost. After the meeting was over certain group members spoke to me and tried to explain about established custom and practice in the Labour group for making nominations to elect a candidate for the mayoralty. Every year two names were proposed, and according to custom, the winner of the contest became the mayoral candidate and the runner up is usually nominated and selected the following year. This would mean that I would be favourite to win the nomination the next year.

The following year I talked to my supporters and tried my best to persuade them to abandon the idea of proposing my name for a second time. I thought about my position in the Labour group if I lost the contest again. I posed certain questions to them, for example, what would happen if I lost again at the vote if the normal custom and practice was not followed for any reason. If this happened, I asked them, what would be my position as a member of the Labour Group? They were, however, determined to go ahead and push my name for nomination. And so once again, at the Labour group meeting in November 1984, my name was proposed and, as expected, I lost the contest. I could not see any reason for this failure other than underlying racial prejudice within the Labour group. I decided to bring it out into public domain and issued a press statement, which was printed as headline news on the front page of the *Express & Star*.

It was a very controversial, and indeed courageous move, and I was fully prepared to face the consequences and stand up to any challenge to my views. For me it was not a question of getting a nomination for the mayoralty but a tough fight for equality of opportunity and justice. I was determined to expose the underlying racial prejudice that existed within the Labour Party and its elected members on the council.

This move attracted a great deal of public support and sympathy for me, and my telephone remained a hot line for several weeks. However, my stance no doubt generated some opposition and hardened the attitudes of some of the right wing members of the Labour group. Certainly a number of group members felt bitter and quietly expressed their concern to me whilst trying to prove themselves innocent of the allegations of racial prejudice. They were not denying the facts about underlying prejudice within the group but they were not happy with me for going public about this issue. Some of the group members were also feeling guilty and remorseful about the behaviour of others.

A number of Labour Group members approached the leader of the Wolverhampton Labour Party and pressurised him to take some action against me. They asked him to withdrew the

The Express & Star broke the story of my allegations.

whip and expel me from the Labour group. Subsequently, I had a 'show cause' notice served on me, and was summoned to a meeting with Councillor J. Bird the leader of Wolverhampton Labour Party. We had a reasonably friendly meeting for about an hour and during the meeting he said that the town has never had a mayor from any ethnic minority or denomination other than the white Christian community. He told me that some of the Labour group members worried about losing their seats at the next election if we appointed a black mayor. He warned me that there could be drastic consequences—including even the possibility of losing the control of the council at the next election—and that he was under a great deal of pressure from certain Labour councillors asking him to expel me from the Party or at least withdraw the party whip. I could not believe that some of the so-called left wing socialist councillors had amazingly double standards. I told him *"John, you too are scared of these pale bellied Socialists. I am sure they might have threatened your leadership."* He replied that it was not true but some of them had strong feelings about the issue. I said *"Don't you think their feelings and actions are contradictory to the national policy of equality of opportunity of the Labour Party?"* He said that he agreed with me to a certain degree and expressed a great deal of sympathy for my views. He said that it was not a sensible move for me to raise it in the press and that some of the Labour members and councillors were very upset and deeply hurt by my press statement on the front page of the local paper. In reply I told him that these are not just accusations but factual analysis of what took place at the group meetings. I told him that I stand by my accusations of racial prejudice within the Labour group and was prepared to face the consequences of my public outburst. He smiled and said, *"I know you want to become a martyr but I am not going to let you"*. However, he expressed a deep concern about the negative attitude of some of the group members and that he regretted the treatment to which I had been subjected and he showed a great deal of sympathy towards me. He assured me that he will do his best to explain my feelings to fellow councillors and will do his best to create an atmosphere of mutual understanding.

The following year (1985) saw me handed a most prestigious and responsible role as Chair of the Inner Area

Committee of the Council as well as being nominated to sit on the powerful West Midlands Police Authority. Some members of the group unkindly translated it as a sweetener in exchange of my outburst against the Labour group.

Later that year the time had come again for nominations for the mayoralty for the following year and the leader of the council, Councillor J. Bird, invited me to a private meeting just before the November 1985 group meeting, to discuss the matter. He asked me if I would again be looking for a nomination and in reply I told him yes. Then he asked me how confident was I of success this time, and in reply I said that I am a fighter and do not enter the ring just to win but to fight, fight again and again. He said I admire your confidence and courage. He said the reason I wanted to have a meeting with you is that, as you know that Cllr Purchase is the next parliamentary candidate for the North East Wolverhampton constituency, and if I am prepared to give up my claim this time in favour of him, it would raise his public profile and help him win the seat. He went on to say that he would make sure that I had the nomination for the following year.

It was an extremely difficult decision for me to take as Ken Purchase was my fellow councillor from Heath Town and he was one of my strongest supporters in promoting my campaign for the mayoralty. However, this time I was determined more than ever to test the water and I told him that I do not care about winning or losing but I would become a candidate and my name would be proposed again this time. In the end he wished me a good luck and said don't think that I am pressurising you in any way. My name was once again proposed at the group meeting on 15th November 1985....and this time I won the contest in a secret ballot with a comfortable majority. After the group meeting was over,

Councillor John Bird came across the room and expressed his satisfaction about the outcome of the selection vote. He congratulated me and quietly disclosed that more than two thirds had backed me.

The following day the press printed headlines that Wolverhampton was going to have the first Asian born Mayor. There was a great deal of enthusiasm and happiness all over the town particularly amongst ethnic minority communities. My phone kept ringing non-stop for several weeks congratulating me on the nomination. I was highly encouraged and pleased at the help and support extended by many community organisations and well-wishers from all over the city and beyond. Some of them spoke to me on the phone and in person and others sent letters of best wishes.

At the same time, my political opponents opened old racial wounds, trying to capitalise on the news in order to achieve political gain at the next local election. It was extremely difficult for them to accept that a non-white person would be taking the office of Mayor of the town. Whilst they could not find anything to block my nomination by the Labour party they did dig out some unfortunate arguments several years ago between me and one of the councillors from the opposition party. They took some of the words used totally out of context, and accused me of calling him a bomber and murderer, and applying it to all ex-servicemen, using this very emotive and sensitive issue to tarnish my public image. The opposition party embarked upon a calculated public campaign against me and issued press statements saying that I would be a curse on the town, because I called ex-servicemen murderers and bombers. They carried on with their relentless war and smear campaigns against me for several months. Regular

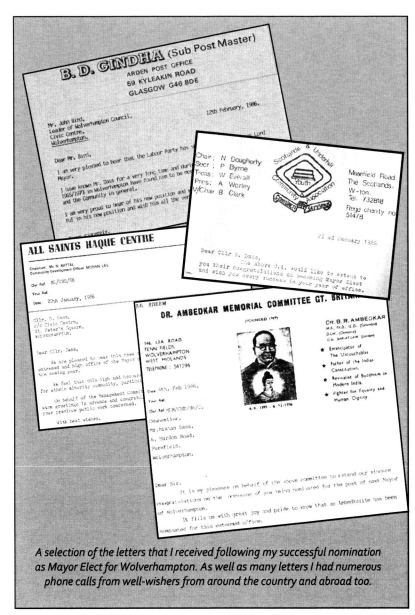

A selection of the letters that I received following my successful nomination as Mayor Elect for Wolverhampton. As well as many letters I had numerous phone calls from well-wishers from around the country and abroad too.

My nomination as Mayor was also reported in a number of newspapers back in India.

श्री बैंस इंगलैंड में पहले अम्बेडकरी मेयर बने !

श्री बिशन दास बैंस

press statements by councillors and members of the opposition party became the norm of the day, with each one repeating the same subject and allegations against me. They even threatened to boycott activities and functions during my year of Mayoralty.

The Tory party were left with no political agenda except repeatedly singing the song of the Mayoralty and they were determined to carry this theme through the local election campaign of May 1986. It was for the first time in the history of the borough of

EXPRESS AND STAR, FRIDAY, JANU/

Fight still on over mayor, say Tories

The Tory group leader on Wolverhampton Council has warned the controlling Labour group that it faces a fight over who will be the next mayor.

Labour has nominated Councillor Bishan Dass as the town's first Asian mayor.

But Councillor Bill Clarke said Labour had to get through the local elections first.

"It is is by no means certain Labour will be in control.

"The electors will make their decision before the mayor is selected at the annual council meeting in May.

"Many people are fed up with Left-wing tendencies and they are facing a rates rise of 50 per cent or more," he said.

It is likely that the Tory nomination for mayor will again be Councillor Dorren Seiboth, who has more than 20 years public service.

Forecast

Labour group leader, Councillor John Bird, hit back at Councillor Clarke's attack over the rates.

"I am glad the Tories are able to forecast what the rates rise will be.

"It seems that are in possesion of more facts than we are.

"I would have thought the indications were that the standing of the Tories at present was so low they would have no chance of taking control," he said.

Councillor Bird said the council had had its books examined and had been told that it operated successfully on behalf of the community.

Meanwhile, the row continued over Councillor Dass's "bombers and murderers" remark to Tory councillor Ray Swatman.

Councillor Dass insisted he made the remark in private, in retaliation for "racist" remarks from Tories.

He said Councillor Swatman, chairman of the Wolverhampton Parachute Regimental Association, should have left the matter in private and not made a public statement.

But Councillor Swatman said today: "I will not accept an insult to the people who fought and those who died in the war.

"Councillor Dass has not apologised to me, as Councillor Bird claims. The only apology I have had has been from Councillor Bird on behalf of the Labour group."

WOLVERHAMPTON CHRONICLE FRIDAY, FEBRUARY 3, 1984

Boycott threat if Bishan Dass elected as Mayor

By Louise Matthews

A TORY councillor says she will boycott civic functions if Bishan Dass, the Labour group nominee, becomes mayor.

Councillor Muriel Hodson has attacked the group's decision, saying they have given in to "blackmail" and reduced the title to a "political football".

But Councillor Dass, who would be Britain's second Asian mayor, has condemned the comments as "nitpicking".

Councillor Hodson said she had received many letters of complaint following the news that Councillor Dass, who last year threatened to resign because he had not been nominated, was chosen to stand for next year's mayor.

"I am not a racist — many of the complaints come from coloured people in my ward," said Councillor Hodson.

"I think the Labour group has given in too easily and are frightened he will resign and take votes with him.

"To be mayor you should have long years of service and have done things for the town. I do not think Councillor Dass fits into either category.

"I will not attend civic functions except for the Remembrance Day parade, but then I wonder if he will, because he voted the people who fought in the last war bombers and murderers."

Muriel Hodson: 'Labour has given in to blackmail'

Bishan Dass: 'It's nothing to do with her.'

"He said that it was because of his colour the he was not nominated last time — is he saying that his Labour colleagues are racist?

"You have only to look at the money they have spent on local area programmes to see this is not the case," she added.

Councillor Dass defended his nomination.

"If Mrs Hodson believes there has been some discrimination here she should take it up with the Commission for Racial Equality.

"But really, this is just nitpicking — what the Labour group thinks really has nothing to do with her.

"Political groups don't consult their opposition when making decisions.

"As for her comments on Remembrance Day I certainly will attend for there were really Indians who lost their lives fighting alongside the British in the last war."

The local newspapers gave considerable coverage to the threat of a boycott by Members of the Tory party.

Wolverhampton that the mayoralty had become a major election issue. They stressed that a Conservative victory on 8th May would ensure a Conservative Mayor—in other words if you vote Labour then Bishan Dass will be the next Mayor and if you will vote Conservative then Doreen Sieboth will become the Mayor of Wolverhampton. They concentrated their efforts on one, and only one, issue—that of the mayoralty and they did everything to divide the community into black and white. Some of their candidates openly played the race card and made unsuccessful attempts to maximise their votes using this. They failed badly and the Labour Party won the local election in May 1986 with an increased majority. Now there was nothing to stop me becoming the next mayor of Wolverhampton and the opposition found themselves unable to do anything to block my appointment. The copy of the 1986 Tory election manifesto printed overleaf is an interesting public document.

The Tory manifesto mentioned the question of who should be Mayor—an unusual topic for an election leaflet.

CONSERVATIVES CARE FOR WOLVERHAMPTON

Social Services

ELDERLY

- Expand home help services.
- Improve standards of social worker training.
- Provide more sheltered housing in co-operation with Housing Department.
- Support provision of nation-wide bus passes for the elderly.

CHILDREN

- Support fostering in preference to Children's homes.

Above all devote money to help people in need in preference to setting up offices and more bureaucracy.

Education

- Provide equality of Nursery School services.
- Insist on discipline and basic education at Primary level.
- Rationalise Secondary education by making necessary economies whilst retaining 6th forms in schools of proven worth.

- Oppose increase in Tertiary Colleges.
- Support improved teacher standards, the GCSE and greater parental involvement in the education of their children.

Published by G. R. Watson 4 Park Crescent, Wolverhampton.

Law and Order

- Support police fully in their efforts to bring criminals to justice and make our streets safe for the public.
- Use new technology and civilian staff to release more police officers for beat duty.
- Encourage "Neighbourhood Watch" schemes.
- Train and equip special units to discourage civil disturbances.
- Press for increased penalties for violent crimes and drug trafficking.
- Support the installation of security cameras in the town centre and increased street lighting.

The Mayor

After 14 years of complete mayoralty we believe that our nomination of Cllr. Mrs. Doreen Swinnerton, with twenty years Council service should take preference over the Labour nominee Cllr. Bishan Dass. A Conservative victory on May 8th would ensure a Conservative Mayor.

Government Aid

The Government recognise the special needs of Wolverhampton by allocating extra money this year and with generous Inner Area grants but they rightly demand efficient use of that money.

COME OUT AND VOTE CONSERVATIVE, THE ONLY PARTY TO HELP YOU OR STAY AT HOME AND ACCEPT 13.4% RATE INCREASES.

Housing

- Tackle the disgraceful backlog of Council house repairs.
- Reduce waste caused by empty houses and horrifying accumulation of rent arrears.
- Expand home ownership and assist first time buyers by selling developments land.
- Stop waste of money on costly areas of offices that rob Council tenants of maintenance.

Value for your money

- Labour's rate increases costs jobs and businesses and private citizens will move out.

The Conservative amendment to Council was to reduce rates below last year's level for the first time in memory.

The Conservative waste not cutting waste not services.

Yes, that's right, you would be paying less than last year.

14 Years of Labour Control—isn't it time for a change?

Printed by J. W. Cooper, (Printers) Ltd., New Cross St. Wednesbury

CIVIC SUNDAY vs CIVIC CELEBRATIONS

Whilst I had won the political battle to become mayor-elect controversy followed me even before my swearing-in. It is customary for the mayor to organise Civic Sunday soon after taking office and to invite town dignitaries, various VIPs, war veterans, and people from various denominations to take part in a service at the St. Peter's church. The vicar of St. Peter's sent me a letter at the beginning of 1986 informing me of the proposed arrangements for the Civic Sunday. In reply I wrote that their will be no Civic Sunday and I will not appoint a Mayor's Chaplain this year. The church leaders of the town were extremely upset and this issue regenerated a great deal of public controversy. They asked for a meeting and I agreed to discuss and listen to their objections. At the meeting they said that it had been custom and practice over the past many years that the mayor organised and hosted Civic Sunday to pray for peace and harmony in our community and that it was now part of the history of the town. We want to preserve the sanctity and maintain the significance of Civic Sunday and that St. Peter' Church should—as always— prepare all the groundwork in advance to facilitate and organise the event.

In reply, I said that whilst I fully understood their position I would be grateful if they could give due consideration to my position as well. The history and traditions that they were talking about were now going through a transitional period where the next mayor of the town was not going to be from one of the indigenous communities. He would be foreign-born and of a different colour compared with the traditional holder of the office. I accepted the historical fact that the majority of residents of this town used to be white and Christian and that they had

77

always had a white Christian mayor but they needed to understand that we now had a diverse community and Wolverhampton was now a very much multi-cultural, multi-faith and multi-racial society where we have people from many different background denominations living in this town. I think they needed to understand that the mayor elect is not a white person, does not come from the indigenous community and belonged to a denomination other than Christianity. The United Kingdom is one of the oldest democratic secular states, and I think the aspirations and expectations of other denominations living in this country deserve to be given equal recognition and respect.

At last, the churches leaders said that they fully understood my position and promised their full support through out my year of mayoralty. I would like to mention here that I had more invitations from churches and attended many functions and services than I did from other denominations and religious places during my year as mayor. On the following pages, I would like to print some of the correspondence I had with church leaders and reaction from the opposition parties.

CIVIC CENTRE, WOLVERHAMPTON

. . .

2853

13 March 1986

POPC

Dear Mr Ginever

Civic Sunday 1986

Councillor Dass has asked me to respond to your letter dated
26 February. Can I begin by drawing your attention to the mis-spelling
of Councillor Dass's name on your letter. I am sure no discourtesy was
intended but equally the mistake could easily have been avoided by
reference to any list of Council members.

I was surprised at the content of your letter for Councillor Dass has
yet to decide what arrangements he wishes to make for Civic Sunday in
1986.

I know that it is normally the case that this Authority's Civic Sunday
Service is hosted by St Peter's but that arrangement has been altered
on several occasions.

Can I ask you to make no further arrangements for the time being until
Councillor Dass reaches a conclusion. Once the Authority has decided
how it wishes to proceed on the matter of Civic Sunday I will immediately
inform you. It may well be that we will seek your co-operation for a
Service similar to that held in 1985 but equally we may wish to make
different arrangements this year.

I am acutely aware of the special relationship which exists between the
Council and St Peter's and would understand your wish, were the Council
to decide not to hold a Civic Sunday Service in 1986, that the Church
should celebrate a similar event, but I do stress that it is premature
to make such arrangements at this stage.

I would be happy to discuss this matter further with you either personally
or by telephone.

I am copying this letter to The Mayor so that he may know of our correspondence

Yours sincerely

(SGD) M T LYONS

The Rev Prebendary J H Ginever
Rector and Rural Dean of
  Wolverhampton
The Rectory
42 Park Road East
Wolverhampton

Principal Officer and
Policy Co-ordinator

MAYOR'S PARLOUR
RECEIVED
1 4 MAR 1986
WOLVERHAMPTON

79

WOLVERHAMPTON
METROPOLITAN BOROUGH COUNCIL
OFFICE OF THE PRINCIPAL OFFICER AND POLICY CO-ORDINATOR

CIVIC CENTRE ST. PETER'S SQUARE WOLVERHAMPTON WV1 1SH
Telephone Wolverhampton 27811 extension 2853
M.T. Lyons B.A. Soc.Sc., M.Sc. (Econ)   Principal Officer & Policy Co-ordinator

'our reference

ty reference   POPC/MTL   2 April 1986

Dear Councillor Dass

Civic Sunday 1986

I spoke last week to Mr Ginever the Rector of St Peter's following
my letter to him of which I attach a copy.

Mr Ginever began by expressing his surprise at my letter, given that
he believes that he was given a clear indication by Miss Saunders that
you were agreeable to Civic Sunday taking place at St Peter's.
This is something I must discuss with Miss Saunders as my discussions with
her indicated a clear understanding that a decision was still to be made
on this matter.

However it was clear from the subsequent conversation that Mr Ginever
has some difficulties in accepting the proposition that:

a) Civic Sunday is the property of this Authority and arrangements will
   be determined by the relevant Mayor.

b) That this year we wish to hold the festival at the Civic Hall. He spoke
   at length on breach with tradition and clearly believes that he has
   personal responsibility in "fighting" to ensure that there is no
   change of venue.

I must stress that I did suggest to him that you would be amenable to
a service taking place at St Peter's organised by the Church, but that
this should not go under the heading of "Civic Sunday".

                                          Continued.........

Councillor B Dass
6 Hardon Road
Parkfields
Wolverhampton
WV4 6HD

- 2 -

Mr Ginever has asked to speak to you personally and I have agreed to convey that wish to you. You may feel that you prefer that discussion to take place in the company of the current Mayor and I would be happy to accompany you should you so wish.

I think this may prove a difficult matter. I do believe that we should concede that the Mayor of the day cannot choose to locate Civic Sunday celebration wherever he or she so chooses. However it is possible that Mr Ginever may seek to make a public debate of this matter given his strength of feeling. I am not convinced that this is a political matter and that Mr Ginever is solely concerned with the spiritual well being of the incoming Mayor or the residents of Wolverhampton. I am copying this letter to Councillor Bird and Councillor Johnson as Chairman of Public Relations so that they are aware of this debate.

Yours sincerely

Principal Officer
& Policy Co-ordinator

METROPOLITAN BOROUGH OF WOLVERHAMPTON

From Councillor: B Bass

6 Bardon Road
Parkfields
Wolverhampton
WV4 6HD

10 April 1986

Dear Bill,

Civic Celebration

I write to bring you up-to-date on the plans I am making for this year's Civic Celebration and to ask for your personal support. I met representatives of the three main Christian Churches this morning and have agreed the following proposals.

I intend, if appointed Mayor, to hold a Civic Celebration in the Civic Hall on a Sunday in either late June or early July (the 29th June currently seems the most likely date). On that occasion I would hope to draw together contributions from the different Churches, Local Industry, the Trade Unions and both sides of the Council. There will also be musical contributions from the Schools Service and perhaps elsewhere.

In addition, I have accepted an invitation from the Christian Churches of the town to attend service on 15th June and would be inviting members and officers of the Council to accompany me on that date. I have also been able to confirm to the Churches that I would, of course, be supporting Remembrance Sunday in November.

I realise that you may not want to respond to this letter until the Council has confirmed its choice of Mayor for the coming municipal year although you will understand my need to make preparations on the assumption that I will be appointed.

Yours sincerely,

Bass

Councillor W E Clarke
138 Pinchfield Lane
Wolverhampton
WV3 6HD

Civic Centre, St. Peter's Square, Wolverhampton WV1 1RG. Telephone 27811

MAYOR'S PARLOUR
CIVIC CENTRE
ST PETER'S SQUARE
WOLVERHAMPTON
WV1 1RG

TELEPHONE Nº 27811

I write to invite you to join the Mayoress and me at the Civic Hall on the occasion of

THE CIVIC CELEBRATION
to be held on

SUNDAY, 13TH JULY, 1986
at 15.00 hours

for which tickets are enclosed.

Wolverhampton is now in the first year of its Second Millenium - a splendid reason for joining together to mark the past achievements of those who founded and fostered the town with investment and jobs through the ages in times good and bad and, of equal if not greater importance, the harmony of the town today and the indomitable calibre of the people who live and work in it.

Harmony is a word closely associated with music so - let us celebrate in music that wider harmony of mankind and, in particular, its application to Wolverhampton.

I do hope you will come and celebrate with me on the 13th July; the programme of music by performers from local schools will represent a kaleidoscope of musical and cultural styles, drawn from the rich and exciting potential of Wolverhampton.

MAYOR
1986/1987
(Councillor Bishan Dass)

Express & Star. 14·4·86

Tory anger over Civic Sunday ban

The decision by Wolverhampton's Mayor-elect to drop the traditionally religious Civic Sunday has been condemned by the Tory leader on the local authority.

Councillor Bishan Dass has announced he will hold a day of celebration in late June or early July at the Civic Hall. He has agreed to attend a church service on June 15 but this will not be the official Civic Sunday service.

Tory leader Councillor Bill Clarke said he was "saddened but not surprised" by Councillor Dass's statement.

"Obviously it won't matter to many Labour members but it does matter to me and my colleagues. And I suspect it will matter to many members of the public who would wish the traditions and practices of the Mayoralty to be maintained.

"Civic Sunday is as much a part of the Mayoral year as Remembrance Sunday, and to dispense with it is a tragedy. We can see the form and dignity of the post being eroded."

Councillor Clarke said there were plenty of opportunities in the Mayoral year for a Mayor to express individuality or to introduce new ideas.

The Conservatives, he said, were proposing Councillor Mrs Doreen Seiboth for the Mayoralty.

"It will take a Conservative Mayor to restore and revitalise the post of first citizen," he added.

Councillor Dass is aiming to invite many people who would not be able to attend the normal religious Civic Sunday. Among those who will be invited will be religious, industrial and local authority leaders as well as trade unionists.

Choirs and bands from local schools and voluntary organisations will provide entertainment at the Civic Hall event.

Councillor Dass has also announced he will be attending the traditional Remembrance Sunday service at St Peter's Church in November.

Chronicle 18·4·86

Mayor-elect replies in civic day rumpus

MAYOR-elect, Councillor Bishan Dass, has defended his decision to drop the traditional religious Civic Sunday.

He said Tory Leader Councillor Bill Clarke's criticisms of the move were "outrageous," and called on him to support a planned day of celebrations at the Civic Hall in June.

Councillor Dass said: "He has not understood my position as a non-Christian trying to represent everybody in the town and not just one section of the community."

He had accepted an invitation from Wolverhampton's Christian churches to attend a service on June 15, but wanted the Civic Hall celebrations to include as many people as possible, he said.

"It would have been disastrous for everybody if I had said I won't go to a church to attend a service. Then the Tories would have had every right to criticise me, but I am trying to take a middle path," said Councillor Dass.

Councillor Clarke said Civic Sunday was part of the traditional mayoral celebrations and should be preserved.

"There has been a tendency by certain mayors in recent years to pick and choose and that is not good enough," he said.

"I do not understand why, if the church service is appropriate, Civic Sunday is inappropriate. Explanations are not due from me but from the Labour group and Councillor Dass."

Despite all the objections I organized the Civic Celebration function at the Civic Hall on 13th July 1986 and fulfilled my commitment and promise made to the residents of Wolverhampton. There were more than four hundred people from many different backgrounds, representing a number of community and religious organisations, the Chamber of Commerce and Industry, trade unions, and VIPs including Christopher Mayfield, the Bishop of Wolverhampton who attended this function. My speech at this event is shown below:

SPEECH AT THE CIVIC CELEBRATION

Bishop Christopher, ladies and gentlemen,
It gives me great pleasure to welcome you all this afternoon to this Civic Celebration. The Mayoress and I are delighted to see you all here this afternoon to celebrate and enjoy the Civic Celebration.
As you are aware, Wolverhampton is in the first year of its second millennium and it give us a splendid reason to remember those who have contributed to the building and development of this town throughout the ages. In addition, and of equal importance, it is a reason to harmonise with those who are endeavouring to bring prosperity and to create an atmosphere of peace and harmony in the community.

But the peace and harmony can only be achieved by paying the price in the form of equality and social justice. It is a well-known historical fact that denial of natural justice and of basic human rights is an open invitation to disturbance, unrest and subsequent violence in our society. Minor issues can add to serious problems consequently posing a threat to peace and unity

As you know, once the German nation was faced with multiple problems of inflation, economic bankruptcy and social deprivation. Consequently, the Jewish community was made the scapegoat for domestic problems and, subsequently, the whole

85

world was dragged into human genocide.

Let us learn from the history and use that experience and know-ledge as a mirror to formulate our future and the future of generations to come. According to an old saying, "prevention is better than cure" and the only real solution to avoiding what took place in the past lies in a mounted attack on every level upon those conditions that breed despair, generate violence, destroy peace and bring nothing but suffering to human being.

We all know what those conditions are: discrimination, ignorance, prejudice, poverty, slums, unemployment, deprivation and health problems. And for the sake of future humankind, sooner we overcome these problems and bring about changes in living conditions for the better. And if we fail to tackle them now, they will remain for evermore a threat to peace and harmony.

Wolverhampton is now a multi-cultural and multi-racial society and the barriers of racial discrimination and prejudice must be ruthlessly eliminated. This nation cannot afford to have situation similar to those now in South Africa. Let us unite to defeat and overcome the problems prevailing in our society....and let us create an atmosphere of mutual understanding, tolerance and unity amongst us.
Let us commit ourselves to make sure that opportunities are available for everyone to progress in life. And let us make sure that the shameful saga of Hiroshima and Nagasaki will never be repeated on this beautiful planet again. Let us make sure that we lay down the foundations and leave behind us a legacy of which the future generation will feel proud. Let us now celebrate......

Tories accused of snubbing mayor

Tory councillors in Wolverhampton were today accused of snubbing the town's new Mayor after members of the 19-strong Tory group failed to attend a celebration at the Civic Hall organised by the Mayor, Councillor Bishan Dass.

Labour leader, Councillor John Bird, said today he deplored the Tories for failing to attend because they were "still aggrieved" at not getting the Mayoralty.

Tory Councillor Phil Turley said today: "It was left to the individual whether or not to attend.

"But the appalling way in which Tory members were treated at the last council meeting finally decided many against attending.

"We felt if he could not be fair to us, we could not be fair to him."

Councillor Bird announced that because the civic celebration had been so successful it was likely to become an annual event.

Enjoyable

Councillors and other community leaders crowded into the Civic Hall organised because the Mayor decided he wanted to have an event in which people of all religions and creeds could join in.

Music, addresses and song made up the theme of the occasion described by one councillor as an "enjoyable and well balanced afternoon."

Councillor Bishan Dass (front left), Mayor of Wolverhampton chats to The Right Reverend Christopher Mayfield, Bishop of Wolverhampton. Looking on are Councillor John Bird (left) and Mr Derek Evans, President of the Wolverhampton Chamber of Commerce and Industry.

THE MAYOR MAKING

At last, the time had come for mayor making ceremony and everything was organised—as usual—at the Wulfrun Hall. There was nothing new about this, the only difference was an increased interest from the press, and there were more people in the public gallery and more VIPs from ethnic minorities than usual. Indeed, there were many more people in the Wulfrun Hall compared with previous years. The Mayor-elect was the focus of attention, as it was for the first time in the history of this town that a foreign-born person was going to take over the role of Mayor of Wolver-hampton. The on-going controversy involving the nomination and other issues had certainly generated extra interest from the press and public alike. The inauguration of myself as mayor took place on 21st May 1986 at the Wulfrun Hall, followed by reception at the Civic Hall. My fellow ward councillor Ken Purchase proposed my name and it was seconded by Councillor Ray Garner and the Tory party proposed the name of Councillor Doreen Sieboth. Voting was by a show of hands which I won by a huge majority and as the results were declared there was huge applause from Labour side, special guests and people sitting in the public gallery. Below is my my speech on this occasion together with some of the press cutting that appeared in the local media.

> May I begin by sincerely thanking Councillors Garner and Purchase for their kind remarks. Since I received the nomination of the Labour Group for the office of the Mayor-ality not all the remarks have been so kind. In the hurly-burly of politics, though, one is used to the odd unkind remark.
> However 1986 is the first time in the history of Wolverhamp-ton when the question of the identity of the following year's

Mayor has become a major election issue. I was flattered to see my name in a prominent position all over the Conservative Party's election address. I wonder if my name had not been Bishan Dass but John Smith or George Howells or Fred Ledsam—I wonder whether in that case I would have achieved such prominence.

I am grateful, however, that the electorate have given their verdict after considering more important and real issues which affect the daily life of everyone in the town.

Above all, of course, there is the tragedy of unemployment. Half of the unemployed in the town have been out of work for over a year. The financial restraints imposed on us by central government limit our ability to respond to the social and economic deprivation in the town. From experience in my own ward I know that poverty compounded by bad housing, a poor environment and unemployment can lead to mental illness, domestic violence and family breakdowns.

In the circumstances I urge everybody in the town including political and religious organisations, the Chamber of Commerce, Trade Unions, voluntary organisations and other caring individuals to become united to work together in order to alleviate these problems.

You know the people of our town are only making moderate demands—the chance of a decent house, of a decent job, of access to educational opportunities, health care and social services. It is a tragedy that in our country—which is still one of the richest in the world—these demands are not being met.

imposed upon it—has already embarked upon a number of projects to meet the needs of the community such as the re-organisation of secondary education, the decentralisation of housing and social services, town centre facilities for youth and expanded leisure facilities for all. I hope that further progress will be made in all these areas in the next year.

1986 is a very important year for a number of reasons:

Firstly, it is a time of hope for all of us as the town enters its second millennium.

Secondly, it is the International Year of Youth. As one of my first acts I shall tomorrow be hosting a lunch to attempt to raise funds for a project which will involve Wolverhampton's young people starring in a film which will be shown on Channel 4 and around the world. The production team were involved in the making of "Gregory's Girl" but the film itself is entirely conceived by our own young people. The film is non-profit making and the Council has already provided backing of £20,000. Hopefully industry and commerce in the town will also provide substantial backing.

Thirdly, it is the International Year of Peace and I urge everyone to play an active part to make sure that the shameful history of Nagasaki and Hiroshima is not repeated on this earth again.

Fourthly, it is Caribbean Focus Year. I want to build on this concept in our town and make it Anti-Racist Year here in Wolverhampton.

Racism is one of the most invidious evils in our society. It divides working people who need to struggle together to improve their conditions. It is the last resort of the ignorant and frightened. I call upon all organisations in the town—whether black or white—to promote events in the next year designed to increase harmony in the community and to banish racism. It will be my intention to attend as many functions and activities as possible and to make myself available wherever my presence will help to promote the cause of the town.

Fifthly, it is Industry Year—I fear that without substantial changes in government policy the revival of industry in the West Midlands will be a slow process. Meanwhile it is the policy of this Council to make it a priority to maintain and develop our existing industries. I will do everything in my power to help in this process.

Wherever I go I shall be determined to carry two things with me in my mind. Firstly I shall be representing Wolverhampton and all of its people. I am glad to be able to announce that the Christian leaders of the town have agreed to participate in a service for the Mayor during my term of office. As for Civic Sunday itself—this year the event will take place in the Civic Hall and many sections of the community will be involved.

Secondly, and most importantly, I shall remember my political and moral beliefs without which a person in public office is arid. The influences on my life have been many—the teachings of my guru Dr Ambedkar who struggled so hard for the poor and deprived people of India; the struggles

91

of the trades union movement and the policies of the Labour Party. All these seem to me to point in the same direction— the promotion of equality, liberty and fraternity. My wife, my family and I shall be delighted to try and promote these ideals in Wolverhampton over the next year.

Asian mayor is elected over Tory opponent

Wolverhampton's first Asian Mayor has been elected.

The choice was made despite Tory moves to promote an alternative candidate.

The election of Councillor Bishan Dass came after a row last night at the annual council meeting over Labour's 15-year hold on the mayoralty.

He was picked ahead of the Tory choice, Councillor Mrs Doreen Seiboth by 37 votes to 19.

During his Mayoralty, Councillor Dass aims to promote good relations between all groups and to see a sense of pride reflected in the town.

He told the annual meeting that for the first time in the town's history the question of the mayor's identity had become a major election issue having figured prominently in Tory election addresses.

The electorate though, he said, had given their verdict after considering more important and real issues affecting the daily life of everyone in the town.

Caribbean

He said Government constraints had affected the authority's ability to react to social and economic deprivation.

"In the circumstances, I urge everybody in the town to become united to work together in order to alleviate these problems," he said.

He aims to work for International Year of Peace and Year of Youth this year and wants to build on Caribbean Focus Year locally by making it "anti-racist" year in the town.

Tory leader Councillor Bill Clarke promoted the nomination of Mrs Seiboth, who has been on the authority 31 years and is married with one daughter.

He attacked the Labour group's attitude of believing it had a "divine" right to the mayoralty having held it for 15 years.

But Labour leader Councillor John Bird pointed out that since 1848 when the borough came into being, the Tories had claimed the Mayoralty more than 100 times.

There had been no agreements between political parties, nor was there likely to be, on sharing the mayoralty, he added.

The new Mayoress is Councillor Dass's wife, Ram Pari.

Councillor Bishan Dass has the chain of office adjusted by Mayor's Attendant Paul Al...

EXPRESS AND STAR, THURSDAY, MAY 22, 1986

THE BIGGEST CHALLENGE OF MY LIFE

After the thrill of the Mayor-making ceremony it began to sink in quite what a job I had inherited. It seemed that I was being attacked from all sides.

There had been regular negative publicity in the local press involving the mayoralty since my nomination with the opposition parties grabbing the opportunity not only to make political gains but also to help to fuel racial tension in the town. But then subsequent to becoming Mayor I started having regular obscene, racial and threatening phone calls, which caused embarrassment and distress to my family. Consequently, I decided to change my phone number quietly but eventually the local press came to know about it. They asked me the reason for changing my phone number and I had to tell them that it was due to some obscene and racially abusive calls that I was having. The local press printed the story and the reasons for changing my phone number. This story gradually found its way not only into the national but also international press. The Indian press in particular exploited the issue totally out of proportion by exaggerating the story. They printed stories that first mayor of Indian origin was having life threatening calls to him and his family. Then following these headlines, I was astonished to receive phone calls from some of my friends and relatives asking me to return to India with my family. I told them that the stories that had appeared in the Indian press were not all true, and they need not to worry about it.

In the Council Chamber itself the opposition parties repeatedly threatened that if the Labour Party imposed Bishan Dass upon them they would never accept him as the Mayor of Wolverhampton. They publically declared that they would do everything with in their power to make his life miserable in the chair at the full council meetings in the council chamber. It was not only a threat but they tried their best to put their words in to practice by adopting unruly behaviour, continuously disrupting the proceedings of the meetings.

Mayor plagued by hate calls

By Tony Halpin

THE first Asian mayor of Wolverhampton, Councillor Bishan Dass, has been forced to go ex-directory because of a stream of racist and abusive telephone calls to his home.

Councillor Dass said the calls had started after his nomination as this year's mayor was announced. British Telecom changed his telephone number less than a week after he took office.

He and his family had been receiving several calls a week, from different people, during the past two months. His 13-year-old daughter usually answered the telephone. Councillor Dass said: "I am used to these things but my family is not. I carried on for a few months but in the end we decided to go ex-directory.

"They said all sorts of abusive things. They are sick people and I am a very healthy person. I didn't want to make myself and my family sick with these abusive things."

Some of the callers had been abusive, others had simply rung his home and kept silent when the telephone was answered.

Sick

"There were different voices and accents. It was quite regular, not every day but certainly every week we got a few calls. The person who answers the phone generally is my daughter. She doesn't upset very easily but she was asking me why people kept ringing up like this," he said.

"My family are not very worried but it caused some embarrassment. Even if somebody rings up and says nothing it makes you feel embarrassed and uneasy. When someone then gives racial abuse on the telephone it is not very pleasant."

Councillor Dass, who represents Heath Town ward, said he had not been surprised by the abusive

Councillor BISHAN DASS — changed telephone number.

callers. But it is the first time he has had to remove his number from the telephone book.

"Being in public life I have gone through all these things in the past and I was expecting much more. I haven't been to the police, I am just ignoring them. They are ignorant, sick people and it doesn't bother me at all.

"I have full confidence in me and in the general public of Wolverhampton, and I expect they will support me. This is only a tiny minority," he said.

Councillor Dass said he had asked British Telecom to change his telephone number before he became mayor, on May 21, but it had taken about a month to do.

But a spokesman for British Telecom in Wolverhampton said: "We normally try to change a number within seven days of the date of request. In this case it took about six days.

"The customer's number has been changed at his request but we are not prepared to discuss any details."

The first meeting of the council was like a tug of war between the opposition and me in chair. It was a real test for me as the custodian of the chair, and I was fully prepared to take the challenge. I was aware of the role and responsibilities of being the Mayor and I was determined to preserve dignity of the chair, and to establish my authority in running the meeting according to the standing orders of the council. They tried their best from the very first minute to practice what they had publicly said they would do by continuously disrupting the meeting and carried on with their unruly behaviour until I threatened to throw out certain members of the opposition party. Some of them were not prepared to give in and carried on disrupting the meeting and shouting across the tables like football hooligans. They continued with their melodrama for about an hour leaving me with no option but to adjourn the meeting for fifteen minutes. I said that I think there is too much heat in the council chamber, and I suggested that every-one go out, have some fresh air, a cup of tea if they wanted one and then come back to the chamber when they thought that they were fit to return. The chief executive sitting next to me, whispered in my ear *"Mr. Mayor, you can't do this, it is against the standing orders of the council".* I said *"You just keep quiet, I am in the chair, I know what I am doing. Don't worry—but thank you for your advice."*

During the break time, I called for John Bird the leader of the council and Bill Clarke the leader of the opposition, into Mayor's Parlour and asked for their co-operation in controlling their members as well as advising them to behave in an orderly manner at the future meetings. I further asked their co-operation in ensuring the smoothly running and management of the council meetings according to standing orders of the council. Both the leaders said that they understand my position, expressed a great sympathy for me, and promised to provide every possible support to conduct the council business in an orderly manner. The council meeting reconvened after a fifteen minutes break and the members behaved better than before and in a more civilized manner. There was one opposition member well known for his racist attitude. He was one of those who created some problems at the first full council meeting. I invited him into the parlour for a drink a weeks after the council meeting. I had a friendly talk with

97

him about his attitude in the council chamber and I said to him that I was not going to lose anything but instead he will have all the negative publicity in the press. I gave him some friendly advice and warned him that if he carried on with his unruly behaviour the press would expose his racist attitude towards me. He smiled and, looking at me, said that you are very crafty. You invited me into the parlour for a drink and gave me lecture on my behaviour in the council chamber. I told him that I was only trying to help him.

Following this members of the opposition party realised that they could not gain anything by behaving in a disorderly manner and that they would damage their own public reputation. Subsequently the council meetings were reasonably constructive and held in an orderly manner for the rest of the year.

Despite all these problems the year as mayor was most enjoyable and one of the most exciting experiences of my life. I attended almost 2300 public engagements of all kinds including political, social, community and charitable events of both national and international importance and I relished speaking at them on a wide variety of subjects. The Mayoress and I had many invitations from cities and towns far away from Wolverhampton. We travelled across the country from the Midlands up into Cheshire, Yorkshire and Scotland as well as south to Bedfordshire and London. I had the honour of having been invited and speak at functions in Birmingham, Coventry, Bedford, Glasgow, London, Nantwich, Bridgnorth, Litchfield, Manchester, Stoke on Trent and Telford. We were a special focus of attention in many places partly because not many people had seen an Indian person as Mayor before and seeing the lady Mayoress going around dressed in a colourful Sari was something of a special attraction to many.

Although there was a great deal of controversy and scepticism in the beginning (particularly involving my ethnicity, political alliance and beliefs) some of the problems were undoubtedly due to a great deal of misunderstanding created by the political opposition and partially through ignorance as people never had an experience of having a first citizen from other than the indigenous community. The opposition, as expected, were determined to exploit the situation and they launched a vigorous campaign to create all sorts of misunderstandings and myths about me and I had a huge task to over come these problems. I readily accepted the challenge and was determined to prove them wrong and show to the people of Wolverhampton that I was a true Wulfrunian and as good as the past mayors of this town. And with the passing of the time, the atmosphere of mutual understanding and trust started to prevail, and the people of this great town started showing an increased interest in the Mayoralty and gave me every possible help and support through out the whole year.

At this point I think that it is appropriate to pay especial tribute to the Lady Mayoress.

My wife could speak very little English and had no experience of public life when she took on the role. She was very introverted and did not enjoy mixing with people that she did not know. She never went to school, as education was not legally compulsory or even a necessity of life in those days in India. Indeed, in the past girls were not allowed to go to school simply due to caste prejudice and prevailing orthodoxy in India. Following my nomination for the mayoralty, we had lengthy talk about her taking over the roll of mayoress. Her first reaction was *"No, no never I am going to accept to be mayoress. What I am going to do there? I do not know anything about it. I have no experience; I*

The Mayor's consort Ram Piari brought charm and grace to the office of the Mayor.

cannot speak or understand English and have never had been involved in such things".

It took me long time— perhaps a few days— to explain to her the role and responsibilities of the Mayor's consort. I told her that she would have every possible help and support and people will be extremely pleased to see a new Mayoress going around in multi-colour sari or in an Indian suite. I had to work hard to build her confidence and persuade her and in the end she reluctantly agreed.

Following this, we started preparations. We went shopping and she bought some new clothes, saris and had some Indian dresses prepared. A few days before the Mayor-making, we went through some rehearsal at the Wulfrun Hall. Although the rehearsal helped build some self-confidence and gave her some idea about what was required of her she was still very nervous during the ceremony. In the hall, she had family and some relatives sitting with her to give her a lots of support. The ceremony for mayoress lasts less than five minutes but she was visibly shaky and nervous. After the ceremony, however, she became more and more enthusiastic everyday. She accompanied me most of the time to various functions and engagements, and always seems to be enjoying every moment. In her colourful sari, she was always the star attraction at any function or gathering that we attended and there was never a shortage of people keen to have a chat with us.

There are certain engagements which by tradition required the presence of the Mayoress only and she frequently she attended these engagements on her own. Her first engagement after taking over the role of Mayoress was to judge the baby of the year and present prizes on 30th May 1986 at the Wolverhampton Civic Hall. This used to be a popular annual event attracting a large gathering as can be seen from the press cutting opposite.

BOY OH BOY!

Little Richard rocks to top of our baby charts

THE bonniest babe in Wolverhampton this year is a boy, the first time the Chronicle Baby Of The Year competition has not been won by a girl.

Winner of class 2, the six-to-12-months section, Richard Siverns romped away with the overall trophy, to the delight of his mum Pamela.

The new Mayoress, Mrs Ram Piari Dass, in her first public engagement, presented mother and son with the silver trophy at the end of a hard day's judging.

The standard of the entries was so high that class one winner, Natalie Jane Blaney, and top class three baby, Hayley Victoria Whitehouse,

Champion baby Richard Siverns, and his proud mother, Pamela, receive the Chronicle Baby Of The Year cup from the Mayoress, Mrs Ram Piari Dass, after the judging.

WOLVERHAMPTON CHRONICLE BABY OF YEAR

tied for second place behind Richard.

Mrs Siverns, of Turnstone Drive, Featherstone, said it was the first competition Richard had entered.

"It is fantastic to win but we will have to see if he wants to enter some more. He's looking very pleased," she said.

Richard, aged 11 months, declined to comment on his success but showed his pleasure by gently poking

his tongue out.

There were 15 smiling young faces in each of the three classes for judges Mrs Gill Brider, from Parasol Photography, Mrs Brenda Platt, a retired nursing sister and wife of the Express and Star personnel manager, and the Mayoress to consider.

Plenty of proud parents and grandparents filled the Wulfrun Hall to encourage their young ones.

In class one, for babies up

to six months, Zoey Louise Partridge, of Oxley Moor Road, Oxley, was placed third. Jonathan Michael Turner, of Quendale, Poolhouse Farm, Wombourne, came second, and top prize went to Natalie Jane Blaney, of Beckminster Road, Penn.

Richard Siverns won class two, for six to 12 months babies, with Daniel Rockley, of Melrose Drive, Lakeside, Perton, placed second, and Rachel Clare Maese, of Grosvenor Road, Ettingshall Park, taking third place to prevent an all-male takeover of the prizes.

The girls took all the prizes in class three, for 12 to 18 months. Jemma Louise Ratcliffe, of Lea Road, Pennfields, in third place, and Juliet Anne Snape, of Ennerdale Drive, Perton, in second, were pipped to the top spot by Hayley Victoria Whitehouse, of Belton Avenue, Wednesfield.

Trophy

Last week's final also saw the return of Hayley Starzak, the 1985 winner. Chronicle editor Steve Gordos, presented Hayley and her mother, Collette, with a trophy to mark the end of her reign as Chronicle Baby Of The Year.

Mr Gordos said the contest had brought together some of the best babies in Wolverhampton.

"They are all winners here and I haven't envied the judges their task of sorting out the winners."

● A bumper bundle of prizes went to the winners and runners-up, donated by Parasol Portrait Photography, Owen Owen, Kinderkurt, W N Sharpe, Golden Bear Products, Babygro, Farley Health Products, Lever Brothers, Start-Rite Shoes, C And A, and Windridge Prams.

Class 2 winner Richard Siverns is seen in thoughtful mood with runners-up Rachel Clare Maese, (left) and Daniel Rockley.

MY YEAR AS MAYOR

While I attended more than 2,300 events whilst mayor there are some in particular that stand out in my mind. I have included a few of the speeches that I made at these events:

DUDLEY ROAD SCHOOL
9th July 1986

"Mr. Chairman, distinguish guests, ladies and gentlemen,
People normally invite the Mayor to perform activities such as cutting ribbons, performing openings, or bringing some good news of hope and happiness.
But today's engagement is just the opposite to that.
We have gathered here this afternoon to commemorate the sad end of a very important chapter in the area's education history, the closure of Dudley Road Primary School.
It is a moment not unlike someone departing from his beloved friends or relatives. A great many people—such as schoolteachers, parents, pupils, school governors, and many others—have a strong personal and sentimental attach-ment to the school.
The Dudley Road School was opened on 9th. June 1873, some 113 years ago, with 29 children, all male on the role. Since that opening, the school has gone through many historical events and has been lucky to survive the destruction of two World Wars.
Over this period a great deal of alterations have been done to the building in order to meet changing educational needs .
As I have said, the school was started with the boys only,

gradually changing to separate boys and girls, and then mixed senior and elementary and, eventually, to its present form of separate nursery, infants and junior.

Unfortunately, this historic establishment, after having gone through all the changes and serving educational needs of the time, Now is to cease functioning as a school. However, although educational activities will have ended, I am sure that it will long be remembered as a landmark in local education for many years to come. Many people will have different reasons for their memories. Many teachers, nursery nurses, cleaners, caretakers, dinner ladies, crossing wardens and others who had provided valuable services in its life, all will have good memories of the school.

However, whilst the school will now close and the children will move to neighbouring schools the building will remain here and, hopefully, for a considerable time. You may be aware that a number of people and organisations are bidding for the future use of the building and the local authority has quite a few suggestions on board. I am sure that we would like to see the fullest possible community use of this historic building and, who knows, it may yet be here another century or two.

Finally, whilst this is a sad occasion in many ways I would remind you that past years have seen considerable achievements, and may those memories remain with us all for a long time in future. In the end, once again many thanks for coming along for the event and I hope, it will not be the last one."

OVERSEAS DOCTORS' ASSOCIATION AGM
6th September 1986 at the Kingfisher, Wall Heath

"Mr Chairman (Dr M.Passi), Dr Chatterjee, Dr Admani, Dr Ball, Ladies and Gentlemen,
Thank you very much for inviting us to the AGM of Overseas Doctors Association I and the Mayoress are delighted to be with you tonight. I have been informed that this is your fourth. AGM and you now have 80 members in your organization, from Worcester and Shrewsbury to Wolverhampton. On behalf of the residents of Wolverhampton, I am grateful for providing laudable professional services by the members of ODA and indeed other overseas doctors to people living with in the area.
The medical professionals like doctors and nurses had a great responsibility and very important role to play in community services. In addition, it is through your professionalism and hard work you have earned a good name as being a backbone of the NHS. Britain is now a multi culture and multi racial society, doctors, and nurses from Black and Ethnic Minorities are playing a vital role in our society. People often say that the public services like the NHS, public transport and the metal industry without black workers would be crippled.
The workers from ethnic minorities have made huge contributions to the economy of this country through hard work, and provided an unchallenged proof of their honesty and loyalty to this country. It is a tragedy that their importance often goes unnoticed and they are subjected to indignation, discrimination and racial prejudice. They are denied equality of opportunity and are provided with less favourable treatment in their daily life. Unemployment in

they are subjected to live in houses unfit for human beings, consequently leading to poor health. All these circumstances are leading to ever-increasing pressure on public services including the NHS. Therefore, doctors and nurses are under enormous pressure. I like to thank you for your most valuable contributions in providing most needed services to the residents of our town. The people of Wolverhampton appreciate the work you are doing and I hope you will continue to do so.

Last, but not the least, I wish you all the best wishes and thank you once again for inviting the Mayoress and myself.

A night to relax

The Wolverhampton Division of the Overseas Doctor's Association met for its annual dinner (its fifth to date) at the Kingfisher Club in Wall Heath on Saturday 6th September.

And what a splendid dinner it was! After Grace by Association President Dr. Chatterjee OBE, and such delights as "Sole Mornay" and strawberries and cream, toast followed loyal toast and witty and welcome speeches were heard

from National Chairman Dr K Admani, and guest of honour Dr J.J. Ball from Kidderminster and the BMA. Mr Cox, consultant gynaecologist and obstetrician at New Cross spoke good humouredly on the varied role of today's G.P. to the enjoyment and approval of all.

With Mayor Bishan Dass and his charming wife also present as guests of the O.D.A., the evening was a tremendous success and

the assembly rose to its feet as one person to applaud Secretary Dr Mohammed Rahmen for his meticulous planning and organisation of the occasion.

Dr Rahmen is a resident of Tettenhall as is Doctor Verma, the Wolverhampton Division's vice president. Other Tettenhall members at the dinner were Dr Baghijani, Dr Ram, Dr Zaman, Dr A Patel, and Dr Gopal.

The annual dinner of the Overseas Doctors Association proved to be a splendid affair.

ANNUAL METHODIST CONFERENCE

"*Mr President, Bishop Christopher, Ladies and Gentlemen,
Today we must thank Mr Gilson for bringing about this
happy gathering for when he was made President of the
Methodist Conference that appointment provided the best
of reasons for the town to celebrate in modest fashion, the
achievements of a modest man which, during his time in
the ministry have been more than a modest few.
It is a fact that Nigel Gilson has total commitment to multi-
racialism, both within and outside the church.
Indeed, it is no coincidence that the first non-white Vice-
President of Conference is a member of the church within
Mr Gilson's district—that is but one example of the way in
which he has encouraged the immigrant community within
the church to develop its full potential.
Nigel Gilson spent many years in Rhodesia working for the
cause of racial integration. He was persona non grata
during the Smith regime and could not have returned to the
country during that period but, happily, since Zimbabwe
came into being he and his wife have been able to visit old
friends there which I know has given them great pleasure.
Mary Gilsdon has worked solidly alongside her husband,
committed to the same cause and imbued with equal depth
of feeling for the common good of all people. What a partnership—supportive in every sense of the word.
This year has seen the 200th anniversary of the Methodist
Missionary Society—how appropriate then that the man
made President of Conference 1986 was Nigel Gilson, for
he was a missionary and comparatively few presidents
have been missionaries. Perhaps those who were the latter
did not survive to become the former!*

My final words to you, Mr Gilson, will be a tribute on behalf of Wolverhampton. During the past 12 years of your ministry to Wolverhampton & District you have earned the respect and affection of the community and the town feels that the Presidency in a very real sense is a mark of your success in that overall ministry. I understand that last year yours was the only district in British Methodism to achieve an increase in membership.

There is one sad note today. Within the space of two years or so Nigel Gilson will cease to be Chairman of Wolverhampton & Shrewsbury Methodist District. So, to him, I say thank you, Mr President, for your years of friendship and your honest concern for the people of this town. We have been fortunate in the far-reaching effects of a first-rate ministry, the result of unflagging enthusiasm and   determination of a first-rate man from whom we could all learn much about that vital art—COMMUNICATION.

Bishop Christopher, Ladies and Gentlemen, I ask you to stand and toast the health and the deserved happiness of Nigel Gilson."

Respect overshadows abuse — Mayor—

Bishan Dass — "Try to keep dreams alive."

WOLVERHAMPTON's first Asian mayor says in his New Year's message "I feel like I belong to the people of this town despite being the target of racist abuse."

Since being elected into office last May Councillor Bishan Dass says he has received abusive letters, telephone calls, and taunts from a racist minority as he travels to his civic engagements. But he calls for the different races in the town to unite to overcome the many problems people are facing, and to spread the message of equality, liberty, peace and hope.

He says: "Since I took over this office I have been subjected to all sorts of racist abuse. I receive abusive letters and even had to get my telephone number put on ex-directory to avoid nasty calls.

"Even when we have been driving along in the mayoral car, some people shout and swear at us — it's all very embarrassing, but they are only a small minority.

"But many people give me a lot of respect as the first citizen of Wolverhampton. In fact, we have been a focus of extra attention when we have attended events because not many people have seen an Asian Mayor and Mayoress before.

"Some people are delighted and some are surprised, and it all gets more attention for Wolverhampton."

He says that this focus of attention is exactly what he wants because if the town comes under the spotlight, some of the problems facing the area might come to light.

"Wolverhampton is faced with high unemployment, particularly among the young, declining industry and few job opportunities," he says. "But I don't think much will change unless central government's policy changes. Our hands are tied unless more resources are available.

"There is nothing we can do as a council except to try to maintain the existing level and support job initatives. We have so many problems, but the only way we can overcome them is by continued struggle and co-operation between the people of different races in the town.

"With the New Year comes hopes and opportunities. Although we are living in hard times, I wish the people of Wolverhampton good fortune in the coming year — they must try to keep their dreams alive."

The local newspaper was keen to report on the change in attitudes and I used my New Year's message to emphasise this.

Dunstall Henge: world meeting in Wolverhampton

— by Stuart Crees —

DUNSTALL HENGE, a sculpture dedicated to world peace, was formally handed over to the Mayor of Wolverhampton, Cllr. Bishan Dass, on October 30th. The sculpture, set in a community park in Dunstall, to be known as Peace Green, is similar to the familiar henge shape, but with a tunnel leading up to a stage area rather like a Greek amphitheatre. It is hoped that it will in fact be used for musical and drama performances.

The venture sets a precedent as a collaboration between a regional arts association, a municipal gallery, a planning department, a school and a local community. The handing-over ceremony took place in the presence of the sculptor, Avtarjeet Dhanjal, Cllr Bishan-Dass and his wife [illegible]. Avtarjeet commented: "The [illegible] was there, and the city council seemed very happy."

Except for the cutting of the stone, all the work was done on site, but Avtarjeet was based at Valley Park School, where he consulted teachers, pupils and community leaders about the work. He describes the school as: "A gateway to the community I was working in. Valley Park helped a lot."

Like a lot of his earlier work, his original concept was concerned with inner peace; the theme of world peace grew out of his talks with the community. He worked with Inter Faith, an organisation of a variety of different religious groups. Although the site has no particular religious significance, he hopes people will find there the serenity of a church, mosque or temple. The tunnel to the stage narrows briefly, a physical metaphor of "A moment to reflect."

Many people in the community carved their names in bricks used decoratively around the site — pupils, adults, and the unemployed youngsters who helped him with the physical labour. He hopes to use more of the bricks next year, working with the same youngsters, to construct a play area in the woods of the park.

On one brick, a woman had drawn a map and written: many nations, one world, many meeting in Wolverhampton.

Sculptor Avtarjeet Dhanjal (left), with the Mayor of Wolverhampton, Cllr Bishan-Dass and the Mayoress at the ceremony to officially open Dunstall Henge. *Photo:* [illegible]

period through lack of maintenance by the Council and eventually part of the structure became a health risk to the public and had to be   removed. The stone with a peace massage survived despite further   damage from vandals and is still intact in the park, but requires some repairs.

However, during my time as Mayor I was pleased to have established peace links with many countries including Australia, Canada, India, China, Japan, Russia and many more. I had several massages of goodwill and greetings for setting up a Peace Green both from home and abroad which had been sent by many distinguished persons representing national and international organisations such as Rene Short MP, Shridath Ramphal (the Commonwealth Secretary), Vladimir Karpenko who was the Chairman of Volgograd Regional Peace Committee, and Valentine Boykova of the Volgograd Regional Friendship Societies Board. Amongst others. I have the pleasure to print some of the most important historical documents and letters pertaining to the peace agenda on the following pages.

MAYOR'S PARLOUR
CIVIC CENTRE
ST PETER'S SQUARE
WOLVERHAMPTON
WV1 IRG

TELEPHONE N? 27611

MESSAGE from THE MAYOR

I greet the peace campaigners of the town and wish you every success in your initiative to build a caring and just world.

Forty years ago, the major nations sat down around the conference table, weary from years of war, to build a new future: their dream was to make a world free from war and from the horrors of poverty and deprivation.

Their task was a hard one, the job of re-shaping the way we live arduous - but, forty years on, many dedicated people are still forging the way ahead in groups sponsored by the United Nations at their headquarters in Geneva and New York.

Lasting world peace is not cemented by protocol - it comes from the heart of ordinary people, for it is they who suffer should world leaders decide to turn to the ultimate crime of war and they are the ones to build the real foundation for peace.

May the peace-loving nations of the world never lose their energies to turn from armament to development - and to change the sword into the ploughshare.

Bishen Dass

MAYOR 1986/1987
(Councillor Bishen Dass)

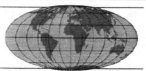

THE MILLION MINUTES OF PEACE
AN INTERNATIONAL APPEAL

International Co-ordinating Office: No. 4, 95 Avenue Road, St John's Wood, London NW8 6HY
Telephone: 01-586 6677; 01-586 9338. Telex 295441 BUSY. Ref. Million Minutes.

**International
Year of Peace 1986**

The Mayor
Wolverhampton Borough Council
Civic Centre
St Peter's Square
WOLVERHAMPTON WV1 1RE

MAYOR'S PARLOUR
RECEIVED
18 AUG 1986
WOLVERHAMPTON

8th August 1986

Dear Mr Mayor and Councillors

We write to you on behalf of **The Million Minutes of Peace Appeal
Committee, U.K.**, and on behalf of those already supporting a major
initiative which is now capturing the imagination of many people
worldwide.

To celebrate the United Nations' International Year of Peace, 1986,
a unique project is being organised to unite people across the world for
peace. The Million Minutes of Peace Appeal is a global project taking
place in over 40 countries, between September 16 and October 16.

The Appeal is somewhat unusual in that it is not a charity, nor a fundraising event, but an Appeal for donations of time. It takes no political
stance, rather it aims to increase people's awareness of the International
Year of Peace, of peace as a personal responsibility, and of the need
to create an atmosphere of peace at a community level.

The Appeal is universal, people of any age, background or belief can
take part and donate through their positive thoughts, prayer or meditation.
A special leaflet with a donation form will be mass distributed throughout
the country before and during the month of The Appeal. The minimum
donation – not much to ask – is just one minute of your time.

Many prominent people and organisations are already actively supporting
The Appeal in Britain (please see attached document).

The Million Minutes of Peace Appeal is a unique approach to an issue
of common concern. The response to the project has been tremendous.
A company called Janevale Ltd will direct mail each of Britain's 34,500
schools with the Schools Project Pack. E.T. Heron Print Ltd will print
five million national leaflets/donation forms and Hyphen Hayden
Advertising and Marketing, a London-based advertising agency, have
donated their design and PR services to the national and international
communication of The Appeal.

United Kingdom Appeal Committee Members: The Rev Dr Edward Carpenter, KCVO; Mrs Lilian Carpenter;
Professor Emeritus Adam Curle; Mrs Elinore Detiger; Lord Ennals; Nigel Farrier; Michael George;
The Rt Rev Trevor Huddleston, CR, Brahma Kumari Jayanti; Nikki Malet de Carteret, MA; Bill Oddie.

Major participating organisations and companies assisting (services and facilities only)
Australian Pulp and Paper Manufacturers, Bewster Scott, Brahma Kumaris Word Spiritual University, Child Development
Foundation, Christian Peace Conference, Coles Myer Ltd, Colston Graphics, Dance Aid, E.T. Heron Print Ltd, Friends of
the Earth, Human Unity Institute, Hyphen Hayden Advertising and Marketing, Independent Motels Association, Janevale
Limited, Junior Chamber of Commerce, Oxfam-America, Overseas Courier Services, Planetary Citizens, Progress Press,
Schalline, Simba Print, The Gandhi Foundation, The Image Bank International, United Nations Association.

120

Borough of Wolverhampton

Presented to
Mr.

BISHAN DASS

MAYOR
OF THE
BOROUGH
1986 - 1987

20th MAY 1987

Vote Of Thanks
from Wolverhampton Borough Council

MR. Dass, who was the first Indian born Mayor in the United Kingdom, has undertaken the many and varied duties of the Office with keen interest and enthusiasm and with a desire to foster good relationships. At the beginning of his year of Office he pledged his interest in youth, peace, anti-racism and the revival of industry in the Town. These interests have been reflected in the variety of social engagements, religious services and sporting occasions he has attended. His concern for the welfare of those disadvantaged has clearly been in evidence.

HE performed, or was present at, a number of openings. Among the ones which gave him special pleasure were: new premises for the Wolverhampton Branch of The Samaritans; the Life Cancer Centre Clinic (the first of its kind in the Midands); a 24-hour care and relief service for the Wolverhampton Multi-Handicap Group; a Conference on "Immigration Laws the Community and the Individual"; the Light House Media Centre at the Central Art Gallery;

an exhibition to celebrate one hundred years of Salvation Army Goodwill Work; and the Black Country Trades Fair. He was present at a service to mark the presidency of the Reverend Nigel Gilson (who has connections with Wolverhampton) as President of the Methodist Conference; started the Bob Geldof Run (in aid of the Geldof Appeal and also local charities), launched the Wolverhampton Health Authority Mother and Baby Campaign and unveiled a Civic Society plaque to commemorate the first meeting, on 16 April, 1848, of the Local Council.

IN pursuit of his objective of fostering peace between nations the Mayor was pleased to take a full part in the design and opening of the Community Arts Project "Dunstall Heritage" when he received a sculpture dedicated to world peace, known as Peace Green.

AMONG the many visitors he and the Mayoress received to the town were: the Under Secretary of State for Employment; the Senior Presiding Judge of the Midland and Oxford Circuit; Lord David Ennals, the National

Chairman of MIND; Mr. Norman Willis, the General Secretary of the T.U.C., and many National and Midlands Trades Union leaders; participants from all parts of the country to a conference on Education and Training Policy After 16 "Education for a Change"; and representatives of the British Korean Veterans Association, Wolverhampton Branch. They also received other visitors from America, Australia, Canada, France, India, Jamaica, Malawi, New Zealand, Poland and Sweden, a party of Russian students undertaking a course at Wolverhampton Polytechic and a party of students from 35 countries.

THEY gained much pleasure from events such as the World War 1 Veterans' Re-union, the Wolverhampton Carnival Parade and the presentation of "The Mikado" by the Wolverhampton Youth Theatre (comprising youngsters from local schools) the Sixth Wolverhampton Marathon and the many and varied events undertaken by the Associations, Clubs and Organisations based in Wolverhampton. They have also particularly enjoyed their association with school children in the town.

THE Council also acknowledges the constant support given by Mrs. Dass to her husband and for the quiet and dignified way in which she has undertaken all her duties as Mayoress.

THE Council trusts that the recollection of their successful year of Office will be a continuing source of pleasure and satisfaction to Mr. and Mrs. Dass.

The Common Seal of the Council of the Borough of Wolverhampton is hereunto affixed in the presence of :-

Doreen M. Seibolli

Mayor

Director of Legal and Administrative Services.

The Mayor-making ceremony was—as always—a grand affair with plenty of pomp and circumstance, enjoyed by a large crowd of well-wishers.

A family photograph taken after the Mayor-making ceremony

Congregation at the University of Wolverhampton.

Participating in a charity walk around West Park

Members of Wolverhampton Borough Council 1985

Visitors on an exchange visit fro Jonesborough, Arkansas, USA

Electioneering for Pat McFadden with Tony Blair in the 2010 election

A meeting with Alan Johnson MP, former Home Secretary and Education Secretary

Receiving a framed photograph from the Mayor of Bridgnorth

Greeting Mrs Rene Short, MP for Wolverhampton NE at the reception at the Council House

Greeting Bill Clark, leader of the Conservative group on the Council and his wife

Receiving the Mayor of Dudley, Cllr Bradley.

Greeting Brian John, Mayor of Walsall

Greeting John Bird MEP and leader of the Council together with his wife.

A recent photograph showing three generations of my family.

OUT OF DARKNESS COMETH LIGHT

Wolverhampton Groups for Peace

Secretary: Mrs M. Chamings
24 Pool Hayes Lane
Willenhall
West Midlands WV12 4PU.

Telephone: Willenhall 67548

11.5.86

Dear Sir,

At a recent meeting of Wolverhampton Groups for Peace the following resolution was unanimously agreed and I am asked to send it to you with the request that it be considered by the Council:

"Wolverhampton Groups for Peace calls upon Wolverhampton Borough Council to take an initiative in seeking to form a friendship link with a town of similar size to Wolverhampton in the Soviet Union. The meaningful relationships which could grow out of such a contact could help to increase understanding between the 'ordinary' people of East and West. As a declared Nuclear Free Zone, Wolverhampton Metropolitan Borough Council might justifiably use resources earmarked for Civil Defence in developing this link for the reason that the best form of defence for the people of Wolverhampton is to actively promote mutual understanding as the surest way of preventing an outbreak of hostilities between ourselves and the Soviet Union."

Yours faithfully,

Margaret Chamings

Margaret Chamings
Secretary.

The Chief Executive
Wolverhampton Borough Council
Civic Centre
St Peters Square
Wolverhampton.

Dear Councillor Dass,

We were very pleased that you came to our IYP Committee last Wednesday. I am sending you this photocopy of the Groups for Peace resolution being sent to the Chief Executive. We hope you will feel able to give your support to the idea of a Friendship Link between Wolverhampton and a Soviet town of comparable size.

Yours sincerely,

Margaret Chamings

OFFICE OF THE MAYOR

THE CITY OF HIROSHIMA

Takeshi Araki
Mayor

August 6, 1986

Dear Sir / Madam:

Today, on the occasion of the forty-first anniversary of the atomic bombing in Hiroshima, we solemnly conducted the 1986 Peace Memorial Ceremony in front of the A-bomb Memorial Cenotaph at Peace Memorial Park. In the presence of Minister for Health and Welfare on behalf of Prime Minister of Japan and many other distinguished guests from within and outside the country, I have read the Peace Declaration which you will find enclosed.

The Peace Declaration conveys our prayer for the repose of the souls of the victims of the atomic bomb and our ardent appeals for the realization of world peace.

This year has been designated as the International Year of Peace by the United Nations. It is of great significance that following the last year's "1st World Conference of Mayors for Peace through Inter-City Solidarity," "'86 Peace Summit in Hiroshima" is being held this year with the participation of Rt. Rev. Desmond M. Tutu, Nobel Peace Prize laureate and other distinguished guests who have deep concerns toward world peace, and that an active exchange of opinions is given to the attainment of world peace, our common goal.

I would like to take the opportunity to renew my deepest respect to you and to all who devote themselves to the attainment of world peace. I sincerely hope that you will kindly take every opportunity to have the meaning of the Spirit of Hiroshima widely understood by as many people as possible.

The Peace Declaration is sent to you with my very best wishes for your continued success.

Yours very truly,

MAYOR'S PARLOUR
RECEIVED
1 3 AUG 1986
WOLVERHAMPTON

Takeshi Araki
Mayor

The City of Hiroshima

PEACE DECLARATION

August 6, 1986

Peace. That is the fervent prayer of the people of Hiroshima.

Forty-one years ago, on August 6, 1945, Hiroshima was devastated by a scorching flash of light and an earth-shaking explosion. The streets were massed with people, many of them dead almost instantly, and many of the rest wondering if death was not the kinder fate. It was truly an earthly inferno surpassing imagination.

Risen from its ruins like the mythical phoenix, Hiroshima has repeatedly appealed for the total abolition of nuclear weapons and the creation of lasting world peace so that the evil not be repeated.

For a brief interlude beginning last August 6, a new age of nuclear disarmament appeared to be dawning as the Soviet Union announced a moratorium on nuclear testing and summit talks between the United States and the Soviet Union were resumed. However, little progress has been made in these nuclear disarmament negotiations. Instead, the world's nuclear arsenals continue unabated their quantitative and qualitative expansion, accompanied now by a dangerous new nuclear strategy that would extend the risk of atomic bomb holocaust into space.

The Soviet nuclear accident at Chernobyl brought the people of the world face to face with the horrors of lethal radioactivity, arousing serious concern about the lack of mechanisms for international controls and cooperation in case of a nuclear power plant accident. The world shuddered as it witnessed the reality of our nuclear age — the ease with which a nuclear disaster in one country can spill its deadly contamination and consequences into other countries.

Compounding this, regional conflicts and terrorism have become increasingly commonplace, and peace suffers from the growing specter of starvation, the plight of refugees worldwide, the denial of human rights, and other affronts to human decency.

Not long before he was so tragically felled by an assassin's bullet, Sweden's Prime Minister Olof Palme visited the Hiroshima Peace Memorial Museum. Seeing the human shadow imprinted on the stone steps by the scorching heat of the atomic bomb, he remarked apocalyptically that a nuclear war now would probably erase even the shadows on the stones.

When the members of the Nobel Peace Prize-winning International Physicians for the Prevention of Nuclear War visited Hiroshima this June, they were aghast at the historical record and moved to issue a vigorous appeal for an immediate halt to all nuclear testing.

Today, Hiroshima Day is being observed in cities and towns around the world. In Mexico, for example, the heads of state and government of six non-aligned nations are meeting together to appeal for nuclear disarmament.

Calling for the total abolition of all nuclear weapons and the attainment of world peace, the voice of Hiroshima is today the voice of all peoples everywhere.

There is no time to lose.

The nuclear powers should immediately and permanently halt all nuclear tests. Holding the fate of all humankind in their hands, the United States and the Soviet Union should hold a summit meeting in Hiroshima City — both victim and survivor of the world's first atomic bombing — and take the first practical steps toward nuclear disarmament.

We strongly and respectfully request the Secretary-General of the United Nations to urge the leaders of the United States and the Soviet Union to visit Hiroshima, and we further request the Secretary-General to take immediate action to convene the Third Special Session of the United Nations General Assembly Devoted to Disarmament.

In keeping with the ideals of peace embodied in the Constitution and steadfastly adhering to the three non-nuclear principles, the people and government of Japan should take the initiative in leading efforts for the elimination of nuclear weapons and the attainment of world peace.

This year has been designated the International Year of Peace.

We are holding this Peace Summit in Hiroshima today to mobilize the world's conscience for the total abolition of nuclear weapons and the attainment of lasting world peace.

Hiroshima repeats its appeal.

It is essential that all cities and citizens of the world join together in expanding the circle of solidarity transcending national boundaries, partisan ideologies, and religious creeds to strengthen the bonds of human friendship and solidarity.

Today, on the occasion of this ceremony marking the forty-first anniversary of the atomic bombing of Hiroshima, we offer our prayer for the repose of the victims' souls, request that the government of Japan enhance its relief measures for survivors and bereaved families alike under the principle of national indemnification, and rededicate ourselves anew to the cause of peace.

— Delivered by Takeshi Araki, Mayor of Hiroshima City

LIGA FÜR DIE VEREINTEN NATIONEN
IN DER DEUTSCHEN DEMOKRATISCHEN REPUBLIK
(Mitglied der Weltföderation der Vereinigungen für die Vereinten Nationen)

UNITED NATIONS ASSOCIATION
in the German Democratic Republic
(Member of the World Federation of
United Nations Associations)

Otto-Grotewohl-Straße 19 D
Berlin
1086
Fernruf 2 29 10 27
Telegrammadresse: UNO Liga Berlin
Bankkonto: BSK 6651-32-659

Message

On occasion of the UN-Day the United Nations Associations of the German
Democratic Republic send their cordial greetings to the audience of the
festive session in Wolverhampton.

This year the United Nations Day is of special significance being
incorporated in the International Year of Peace.
Only if peace is translated from many declarations and resolutions into
practical actions is there a chance to save coming generations from
the scourge of war.
Among them, the unilateral moratorium on nuclear explosions is one of
the most substantial. This is precisely the kind of action that proves
the sincerity and responsibility for the future of mankind.
The problem of nuclear testing puts in sharp focus the two mutually
exclusive approaches. One can imagine the sigh of relief that people
would have on hearing that in this Year of Peace the United States, too,
has decided to stop nuclear testing.

We from our side urge all peace-loving forces to do the utmost to
save our children and grandchildren, and indeed all people on our planet,
from a nuclear catastrophe. We cherish the ideal of a world without war
and without weapons.

Please join us to make this vision a reality.

Felicitas Richter
Secretary General

124

HOUSE OF COMMONS
LONDON SWIA OAA

I have always supported international relations between countries and nations. I condemn warlike activities wherever they come from and I condemn terrorism of any kind whether exercised by individuals, organisations or states.

I have always been a supporter of CND and I initiated the "Women in Black" movement in the sixties.

There are some 50,000 operational nuclear warheads in the world today. These could unleash unspeakable suffering and destruction on all living beings on our planet.

I strongly support the proposals for the reduction in nuclear armaments put to us by Mr. Gorbachev when the Parliamentary delegation of which I was a member met him recently in Moscow. I hope all Wolverhampton citizens will do the same. "Peace is indivisible".

Renée Short

16. IX. 86

OFFICE OF THE COMMONWEALTH SECRETARY-GENERAL

MARLBOROUGH HOUSE · PALL MALL · LONDON SW1Y 5HX   23 October 1986

Message from the Commonwealth Secretary-General on United Nations Day - UN International Year of Peace Celebration in Wolverhampton

As you celebrate United Nations Day in this International Year of Peace, I send you warmest greetings on behalf of the Commonwealth: a Commonwealth of 49 countries whose governments and peoples recognise that peace and development are indivisible in our interdependent world.

We live in a world of infinite promise but one faced by terminal danger; a world which can survive and prosper together or collectively be hostage to self-destruction.

There is an unmistakable and growing impetus for peace and disarmament among the peoples of the world; it is a spontaneous, popular, mass movement - it has a fresh and compelling vitality.

Your celebration today is part of a global conviction that together we have a common interest in our mutual survival. Today, as we re-dedicate ourselves to the spirit and the ideals of internationalism which inspired the founders of the United Nations, we should never forget that the UN was not created by impractical idealists but by practical men living in the real world and, like ourselves, acutely conscious of our vulnerability to war.

I share the hopes I know you earnestly nourish that we may enter a period characterised by a new spirit of internationalism, keeping faith with the Charter that was signed in San Francisco in 1945. I share with you the longing for a 'new detente' that will stop once and for all the spiral of the arms race and bring not only peace in our time but peace for all time.

In expressing their support for the United Nations, Commonwealth leaders at Nassau called "upon the world community to construct a framework of collective security based on mutual trust and shared interest". "All nations", they said, "have a stake in disarmament. We therefore look for urgent agreement in reversing the arms race and on significant reductions, and eventual elimination, of nuclear and other weapons of mass destruction." Commonwealth leaders invited all peoples and nations to join in a universal effort to fulfil these objectives. You can be certain you have their support for your celebration of United Nations Day.

Shridath S. Ramphal

UNITED NATIONS   NATIONS UNIES

Proclamation

*"The General Assembly
Solemnly proclaims 1986 to be the International Year of Peace
and calls upon all peoples to join with the United Nations
in resolute efforts to safeguard peace and the future of humanity."*
(Resolution 11/1)

from a message to Students of the world
by Senor Pérez de Cuéllar, Secretary General of U.N.0.

Dear Student,

- - - - - - International Year of Peace follows directly on 1985
International Youth Year, a year in which you, a major part of the world's
people, shared the United Nations' concerns about the issues of war and
peace, poverty and development, injustice and freedom.

No one better than you can share and value, understand and
fight for, the ideal of peace and progress. It is you who will inherit
the future. Accordingly, no one has so much at stake, no one has as much
to gain from a more just and harmonious world.

Peace - proclaimed by the *United Nations Charter* as its supreme
objective, cannot be achieved without widespread understanding of the
difficulties preventing a more stable international order. Now, in this
International Year, you can play your part by helping to elucidate the
issues that bear on peace, drawing attention perhaps to the absurd misuse
of resources in a world where two thirds of the population live in hunger
and misery. *The need to limit and ultimately to halt the arms race has
never been more pressing.*

The path of the future remains open. One road leads to peace,
the other can lead to self-destruction. In this critical situation
students of all nations, of all ages, can play an invaluable role,
awakening new hopes and renewing energy in our common search for peace.
The world is listening for what you have to say.

Javier Pérez de Cuéllar
Secretary-General

VOLGOGRAD REGIO AL PEACE COMMITTEE
8, Krasnoznamenskaya Street,
Volgograd, 400036, USSR

ВОЛГОГРАДСКИЙ ОБЛАСТНОЙ КОМИТЕТ ЗАЩИТЫ МИРА

October 8, 1986

Dear friends in Wolverhampton,

On behalf of Volgograd Regional Peace Committee, Soviet-British Society Board, and all the people of Volgograd, we extend to you all across the seas our brotherly greetings!

We live in the hero-city where the historic Battle of Stalingrad took place. The heroes of Stalingrad fell to end the last terrible war for us. And we the citizens of this sacred land in the heart of Russia commit ourselves wholeheartedly to the same common cause with you the citizens of the West Midlands in the heart of England. The common destinies of the first two sister-cities - Coventry and Stalingrad - have served all mankind a lesson that we must have war no more! conventional or nuclear, hot or cold! We cannot afford another war in Russia or England, Europe or America, on this Earth or in the realm of the stars.

Let us not allow so-called 'national interests' or outdated imperial ambitions of any kind to push this globe to the brink of holocaust. Let us help some political leaders adjust to the Nuclear Age reality, accept the new mode of thinking and internationally recognised rules of civilized behaviour.

We are still optimistic about the good start taken by Comrade Gorbachev and Mr Reagan in Geneva and we hope that the meeting in Reykyavik will help break the deadlock in Soviet-American talks. The agreement in Stockholm is a sign of hope for our European home too. But all our effort could be lost, for nothing, if we miss a very good opportunity.

We believe that all of us together still can give peace a fair chance. Let us silence the deadly blasts in Nevada and elsewhere in the world. Let us make Mr Reagan, Mrs Thatcher and Mr Mitterand follow the goodwill examples of the Soviet Union and China. Let us bring our Governments from threats and fears, to talks and mutual trust. Let us join our efforts and win a first victory together. Let us win a Comprehensive Test Ban Treaty now before the Soviet moratorium is over.

The people of Volgograd wish you success in all your challenges for peace and justice.

Long live love and friendship! May there always be peace and life!

On behalf of the people of Volgograd

Vladimir Karpenko
Chairman of Volgograd Regional Peace
Committee

Valentine Boykova
Executive Secretary of Volgograd
Regional Friendship Societies Board

Wolverhampton Groups for Peace

Secretary: Mrs M. Chamings
24 Pool Hayes Lane
Willenhall
West Midlands.

31.10.86

Dear Councillor Dass,

I was away from home for three days this week and so was unable to attend the handing over of the Dunstall Henge peace sculpture. I was very glad, however, that Marjorie Turner was able to be there and I have heard from her that it was a very happy occasion. The invitation to join the company afterwards in the Mayor's Parlour was also awaiting my return last night. I regret I was unable also to accept that.

On behalf of Groups for Peace I would like to thank you sincerely for the excellent message you sent us for United Nations Day. It was duly read aloud in Queen Square on the 25th and has been on public display, along with the 19 other messages, this week in the Civic Centre. We have now collated the various messages into one special Newsletter and I enclose a copy for you herewith. All who sent us messages will be receiving copies of the Newsletters so they will be sent out east and west. We are glad to have been able to make this gesture for United Nations Day in Wolverhampton, and we thank you for contributing so appropriately to it.

Yours sincerely,

Margaret Chamings

Margaret Chamings

Councillor Bishan Dass
Mayor of Wolverhampton
Civic Centre
Wolverhampton WV1 1RG

MAYOR'S PARLOUR
- 3 NOV 1986
RECEIVED

GUJRATI CENTRE WOLVERHAMPTON
Laying the foundation stone on 02.11.1986

Wolverhampton was changing fast during the period of the 1960's because a large number of immigrants from Commonwealth countries came to United Kingdom and many of them arrived here in Wolverhampton.

Wolverhampton was transformed in every respect from an indigenous to a multi-ethnic demographic population, with the emergence of new multi-racial culture and society. The ethnic minority community was now settling down into its new environment, gradually adapting to the new way of Western life and partially overcoming their accommodation and employment problems. Their thinking had changed from considering it to be a temporary stay here for a few years in order to earn some money, and then return to the country of their origin to looking at becoming a permanent residence in this country. They started feeling that they were missing cultural heritage, which had been left behind in their country of origin, and so they eagerly started looking to set up temples where they could get together and fulfil their urge for belonging to their cultural heritage. The largest ethnic population in Wolverhampton was the Sikh community, and they were quick to set up a number of Gurudwaras. Punjabi Hindus were at loggerheads in establishing a Hindu temple whilst minority Ravidassias, Gujrati Hindus, Buddhists and others were looking for to follow in the footsteps of others. In 1986, the British prime minister Margaret Thatcher said that we in Britain are being swamped by foreign culture.

A small group from the Gujrati Hindu community organised themselves, raised some funding to set up their own temple and community centre in Upper Zoar Street in the Penfields area of Wolverhampton. I had good relations with the Gujrati community particularly with their leader Mr Ratti Lal Patel, who used to be a community activist in the town. They invited me as the Mayor of the town to lay the foundation stone of the temple. It was a great honour and privilege and I was pleased to accept the invitation.

On the other hand, I was surprised that they had decided to invite me to perform this noble task in spite of knowing well my background. There was a time in Indian history when people from the Untouchable community were not allowed to worship God and the entry of an Untouchable into a temple used to be a punishable sin for polluting the Hindu temple. A great man like Dr B. R. Ambedkar, the father of the Indian constitution, once entered a Hindu temple in his capacity as minister of the British Viceroy's cabinet and the polluted temple had to be purified with Punchgamani (a mixture of cow ghee, milk, water, cow dung and urine) after he left the building.

I was therefore particularly pleased to be invited to lay the foundation stone of such a historic establishment as a Hindu temple here in Wolverhampton. It represented a great change, new thinking that was fit for a modern society and a significant departure from orthodoxy. It was not only laying the foundation stone of a temple but also the start of the era of a modern civilized society based on equality and liberty. There was a large gathering and many VIPs including Councillor John Bird, the leader of the Council, and I am pleased to print photos of this historical event of the ceremony of laying the foundation stone of the Gujrati Centre in Upper Zoar Street, Wolverhampton

Laying the foundation stone of the Gujrati Centre. On the far right is Cllr J. Bird.

PUNJAB TIMES—1st to 7th MAY 1987-PAGE 11

ਡੂਢਵਲੀਪੱਟਣ ਦੇ ਗੁਰਦੁਆਰਿਆਂ ਦੇ ਪ੍ਰਬੰਧਕਾਂ ਨੂੰ ਉੱਤਰ ਨਾਲ ਲਿਆਂਦਾ

BILSTON CANCER CARE CENTRE

I am life long supporter of the national Cancer Research organisation. I have collected funds and made regular contributions from my own pocket over the past several years to support Cancer Research. An increasing number of people throughout the world are becoming victims of this terminal decease every year and there is hardly anyone who has not lost either a friend or relative or has suffered cancer. I lost my mother to cancer at the age of sixty, and some of my friends and relatives have suffered too. I am proud to be associated with Cancer Research and had the pleasure to provide whatever possible help and support to Life Care Clinic Centre.

A voluntary organisation 'Life Cancer Care Clinic' lead by Dr. Manny Patel, was set up in Bilston and I worked closely with the organisation helping raise cancer awareness, fund raising events and contributed to funds and raising profile of the organisation. I was presented with a facilitation certificate in recognition of this help and support I had provided to promote the cause of cancer relief.

Cancer care partnership

A PARTNERSHIP has been formed in Bilston which will open up a range of advice and care for West Midland cancer sufferers.

At its official opening, Wolverhampton's Mayor, Councillor Bishan Dass, welcomed the new service and pledged a donation from his charity fund.

The Wolverhampton Area Health Authority is supporting the voluntary Life Cancer Care Clinic by giving a consulting room in the Bilston Health Centre, in Prouds Lane.

This will be the base for help and advice on Wednesdays, between 2pm and 5pm, and on Fridays, from 1.30pm to 4.30pm.

It will also allow specialist Dr Manny Patel, a director of the clinic, to continue his work in the treatment of the disease.

The clinic is the first of its kind in the West Midlands and will be run by LIFE, an organisation which has formed close links with health officials.

It is the first time a local health authority has formed a partnership with a completely voluntary organisation.

Staff will be able to offer patients and their families the time to talk about their problems and fears and can discuss aspects of the treatment they do not understand.

The purpose of the clinic is to supplement the work being done by doctors in the field of cancer care, an area which is mid-way between the health services and a hospice.

LIFE has already raised more than £10,000 from fundraising and donations to .... of cancer care but has a target of £30,000 to buy and equip a more ambitious clinic.

Mrs Pam McGregor, one of the clinic's counsellors, says: "We complement the service that a hospice gives and also that of the health services.

"Our counsellors go around the country giving lectures and helping both patients and cancer groups.

"The fact that the area health authority is supporting us as a volunteer group is unique. It shows that we are offering a most worthy service.

"Anyone who needs advice on care and treatment is welcome to come to us. Already we have had inquiries from Sheffield and many other parts of the country.

Attention

"The donation from Bishan Dass is very welcome and is very much needed towards our target of £30,000. This could be used to buy a large premises to accommodate residential patients for a week.

"The project has attracted a lot of attention and I hope it is the beginning of a new move in the care of cancer."

At the opening ceremony, Bishan Dass said: "Cancer is a disease which now affects almost every family in this country and people of all ages. This project will be instrumental in relieving the burden in the minds of patients and their families."

He pledged the support of the local authority in the centre's attempts to open and maintain a residential cancer centre in the West Midlands.

● At the opening ceremony are (from left: Pam McGregor, Dr Manny Patel, Lilian Richards, Mayoress Ram Piari, Mayor Bishan Dass and Jenny Underhill.

The local newspaper reported in detail the opening of the Life Cancer Care Clinic in Bilston.

135

WEDNESFIELD ROTARY CLUB AGM
1st October 1986

I was invited to address the annual general meeting of the Wednesfield Rotary Club. In my speech, I highlighted prevailing problems pertaining to socio-economic conditions of the town:

"Mr Chairman, Gentlemen,
At present Wolverhampton is going through fundamental changes of social and economic structure. It is mainly due to the rapid decline in our production industries and is resulting in ever increasing unemployment and a poor environment.
In about a decade the borough has moved from full employ-ment and a healthy looking economy to massive factory closures and mass unemployment.
There are about 22,000 people now out of work which is 21% of the total workforce as compared to 13.2% nationally and 14% for the West Midlands generally. 51% of the unemployed here have been out of work for more than a year and 37% are under 25 years of age. Parts of the inner areas of our town are suffering disproportionally from this very high rate of unemployment. Some wards like St Peter's and Low Hill have over 33% unemployed and some pockets of the town have up to 60%-70% unemployment.
Manufacturing employment in Wolverhampton fell by 19% during the period 1978 to 1981, a loss of nearly 11,000 jobs mainly in metal and mechanical engineering.
So who are the most affected?
Statistics show that youngsters, the ethnic minorities, women and the disabled are suffering disproportionally from the present economic recession and industrial decline. These groups have not only suffered a disproportionately higher

percentage of unemployment but a high percentage of those who are working are in very low paid jobs.

The whole situation is becoming more serious as there is no sign of improvement. The number of people on Social Security is increasing with 38,000 now on housing benefits and 12,000 children now receiving free school meals.

The whole social and family structure is going through a major change as a result of the decline of our industries, the poor environment, ever increasing long lasting unemployment and the reduction of income and the resulting growing poverty.

Subsequently there is a dreadful increase in the crime rate, an increase in fuel supply cut offs, more broken marriages and a rising divorce rate and an increase in child abuse.

The pressure of unemployment and poverty has generated a feeling of hopelessness, neglect and alienation amongst youngsters which has given further rise to rejection and rebellion against society. In the past society has experienced with grave concern the expression of such feelings on the streets of our towns.

What is the solution then?

The longer term solution to these problems does not lie with oppressive measures such as a heavy handed police force, plastic bullets, heavy fines and longer prison sentences but rather a concentrated attack upon those conditions that generate despair and violence, create poverty and frustration and divide society into the haves and have nots.

According to Lord Scarman the solution depends upon a successful outcome to our current economic problems. In order to secure social stability and proper law and order there will be a long term need to provide useful and gainful employment and suitable housing plus educational, *recreational and leisure opportunities for our youngsters. Therefore there is a need for a co-ordinated approach by local and central government, trade unionists and industrialists to work together in order to achieve these objectives."*

INSTITUTE OF BANKERS DINNER
13th November 1986

"Mr President, Ladies and Gentlemen,
I feel very privileged to be asked to respond to the toast "The
Borough of Wolverhampton" and to add my own remarks
made to the comments made by Mr Kersen.
It is important to realise that the Borough comprises the
widest possible range of organisations and interests. It in-
cludes industrial and commercial businesses of all types and
sizes and these are well represented here this evening.
It includes the Borough Council and other public sector
organisations which provide an extensive network of services
to the public. It includes voluntary organisations, large and
small, which do so much valuable work for the community. It
includes societies, groups, clubs and institutions where
individuals join together in the pursuit of common interests.
Last, but most important of all, it comprises the people of
the town—people with different backgrounds, different
opinions, different ambitions, different problems and
different needs. There is therefore a very wide spectrum of
life amongst us and sometimes—and in some ways—the
interests of certain of the components do not coincide with
the interests of others. There is, in effect, competition—just
as there is competition as the basis of business enterprise in
which you are all engaged. Frequently that competition
between groups in society is healthy or at least without
noticeable ill effect. At other times and in other ways it can
be difficult and divisive. Sometimes the difficulties are
capable of comparatively easily solution but others are
much more intransigent.
It is unfortunately a fact that in many respects difficulties are

shown in sharper relief during periods of severe recession, which at the same time renders other solutions less easily achievable.

That is not to say, of course, that relative prosperity is the answer to everything or that solutions can always be found be economic measures and expenditure, far from it. But there is no doubt that a measure of increased prosperity for business and for the individual does provide a better framework for providing solutions.

Mr President, you and your guests will, I am sure, understand that from my standpoint I see unemployment as the major evil in our midst. 25,000 unemployed would have been unbelievable 10 years ago and is now a reality. I see this in my personal occupation in my work as a councillor and, in particular, as Mayor of the Borough this year.

If there were easy solutions they would have been implemented long since. The Borough Council is attempting to play its part in providing a stimulus to the local economy although its powers and resources are limited by statute. It is, for example, anxious to fulfil as large a proportion as possible of its substantial procurement budget from local suppliers—but obviously in the context of competitive prices.

The Council is also attempting to meet the additional demands placed upon the services it provides—additional demands directly as a result of the economic position. These relate to housing, social services and, of course, leisure services. It is also having to deal with the additional call on social services particularly arising out of increased demand from the changing age structure of the population.

It has done a great deal to improve the environmental aspects of the town and these improvements are planned to continue. Again, there are financial constraints in the level of work that it can undertake.

It is inevitable that there will be differences of opinion about the Council's approach and its priorities—not least of all because its services have to be paid for. The level of rates bills is, to say the least, not popular with everyone. Indeed, I know that a large part of the business community do not think that businesses should pay rates at all.

Frankly, I believe that this view is borne out of frustration and problems arising from the general economic difficulties. I believe that there is much to be said for industry and commerce to continue to bear their share of local government expenditure and that this is infinitely preferable to the Uniform Business Rate which the Government is proposing to introduce in the not-to-distant future.

But whilst on the subject, I would like to emphasise that Wolverhampton's rate poundage is low—almost the lowest of all metropolitan districts in the country. It is the rateable values of the town which are high, reflecting as they do the relative prosperity of the early 1970's. Both the Council and the Chamber of Commerce have both made repeated representations to the Government, to no avail, to bring about revaluation which is 10 years overdue and is costing the town millions of pounds a year in lost Government grants which , as a result, continue to go disproportionately to the South and South East.

I referred earlier to the differences of view which are bound to exist in any dynamic community. These differences, however, must not be allowed to be exaggerated. There is much common ground which should be exploited to the full. And there is certainly one common goal which is appropriate to this evening's toast—that is of the common good of the town and its resurgence.

The Borough Council recognised the point that Mr Kersen refers to when it adopted two slogans "Wolverhampton Working For You" and "Wolverhampton, the pacesetter". These were part of the drive to restore—or if you prefer, improve - the image of the town and to remind the people of Wolverhampton of a common cause and a cause for common pride.

The town is more than the sum total of its constituent parts. It has a character of its own. It has a long and proud history which we must all work to emulate and to secure the future. It is (as Mr Kersen has said) up to all of us. We cannot look for, or expect, a great deal of external assistance.

Mr President, I thank Mr Kersen for his remarks and I thank the Institute of Bankers for allowing me to respond."

GKN TECHNOLOGY VISIT
26 November 1986

In November 1986 I, along with Councillor Inglis and officers from the Council visited GKN Technology, a leading high technology company in Wolverhampton. GKN Technology is GKN's central research and development subsidiary which evaluates technological innovations and adapts them to the Group's needs. It helps other GKN subsidiaries develop new and improved product and advises them on the adoption of process technologies such as Computer Aided Design/Computer Aided Manufacturing (CAD/CAM), robots and lasers.

The tour started in the company's recently opened £3 engineering computer centre which acts as a computer bureau for GKN companies and some of GKN's customers, transmits computerised component designs and specifications around the world and acts as a training centre for GKN engineers in CAD/CAM.

The tour also included the company's testing and development facilities. New vehicle components are tested by machine simulations and by carefully monitored, but gruelling, road tests. Data collected from these tests are extensively analysed by computers and used, with sophisticated software, to suggest changes in design and materials. In this way GKN is able to develop new products into commercially viable products and to improve the efficiency and quality of its many existing products while at the same time minimising costs. This development often takes place with the full involvement of customers.

One new GKN product with far-reaching implications was

its "composite leaf-spring" for use in vehicle suspensions. This is a much lighter and more resilient spring than that used currently in vehicles and therefore helps improve a vehicle's fuel efficiency. "Composite" materials—in the case of the leaf-spring, a mixture of glass fibre and organic resin—are a very important new technology. Increasingly components made of such materials will replace metal in the vehicle and aerospace industry. GKN is in the forefront of this new technology, an important plus for a company heavily committed to the vehicle components industry.

I also visited GKN Technology's Environmental Engineering section which researches into work hazards such as noise, dust, fumes and asbestos and the effects of tool vibration on tool operators. The Environmental Engineering section is also building up a computerised record of the chemicals used in a number of industrial materials such as paint or cleaning fluids, and the precautions that need to be taken if these substances are split, mixed together, mistakenly swallowed and so on.

The visit ended with a description of GKN Technology's training programmes and its "Training For All" policy. Spending on training by the company in 1986 will probably add up to 5% of its turnover. It trains both for its own needs and to produce technologists and technical managers to GKN line companies. It has a large Graduate Development Programme, about half of those on this eventually move on to other GKN companies. GKN Technology also runs a small ETB Engineering Technician scheme and a YTS scheme as well as developing links with schools including providing short placements for teachers in the company and sending speakers out to schools.

ROYAL BRITISH LEGION
8th November 1986

"We have gathered here today to remember brave comrades who sacrificed their lives fighting for justice, liberty and peace on this earth. It is always a sad time of the year.

I pay tribute to their great courage and sacrifice in laying down their lives in order to keep human race going. I am sure that those who died had a fine dream of a future where people of all races and nations could live without any fear of oppression, tyranny and war. And we should continue to fulfil those dreams and it will be our last fitting tribute to them.

Friends, whilst it is a sad time of the year it is also a constant reminder to all of us to play our part to make sure that the shameful history of the Second World War and saga of Hiroshima and Nagasaki is not repeated on this planet earth again.

They have invested heavily in our present and the future generation, and now it is our moral duty to pay their debts by ensuring ever-lasting peace on this earth. Although our sacrifices would not be as great as theirs, we should all be prepared to continue the fight for a better future, where all human beings can live as equals without any injustice, oppression or war.

And let us make sure that all our efforts are focused on investing in saving humankind instead of destroying it. And let us invest our present in the future of our children and their children.

Let us not to forget that those who died for the sake of humankind and the human race had courage to stand up and be counted, and now it is our duty to do the same.

That is the only way we shall be able to fulfil their dreams and pay real tribute to their sacrifice.
Many thanks for your indulgence and listening to me. "

WOLVERHAMPTON POYTECHNIC CONGREGATION
28th November 1986

Wolverhampton Polytechnic was granted University status in 1993 but as a Polytechnic it had a long and honourable history. Over the past many years, it was customary for the mayor of the town to address and chair the congregation ceremonies of the Polytechnic. I chaired a number of ceremonies during my year of mayoralty, and had spoken to most of them. Here is just one of those speeches:

"Mr Chairman, Mr Simpson, Director, Ladies and Gentlemen, I am extremely happy to welcome this Congregation for the Faculty of Arts, Design and Education on behalf of the Borough of Wolverhampton. The achievements of the poly-technic and of its graduates and diplomates bring great credit to the Borough, and the Borough Council is proud of the Polytechnic. The Polytechnic's contribution to the life and well-being of the local community is greater than ever and the Faculty of Arts, Design and Education in particular does much to promote and enhance the cultural, artistic and educational activities within the Borough and the West Midlands region.

The Borough Council and the Polytechnic are engaged in a number of joint projects, such as the In-Service Training of Teachers and the development of a Media Centre, and these are of great value both to the community at large and to the Polytechnic. Through our joint efforts we can more readily achieve educational, cultural and social objectives which might otherwise be difficult to attain.

I am particularly pleased to welcome Mr Philip Simpson,

Head of the Education Department of the British Film Institute, whose advice and encouragement in the development of the Media Centre and in the study of film is much appreciated. I hope, Mr Simpson, that you will enjoy your visit to Wolverhampton. May I extend a warm welcome also to Mr Lashley and Mr Wright who are to become Honorary Fellows of the Polytechnic in recognition of their achievements and as a mark of the esteem in which they are held.

I welcome also the finalists today with their families and friends. I congratulate you on your success and wish you well in your careers. Students come to the Polytechnic not only from in and around Wolverhampton and the West Midlands but also from all over this country and from overseas. I hope that in years to come you will be as proud of Wolverhampton and of the Borough as we are of you.

VICTIMS OF CRIME

Wolverhampton once used to be regarded as the heartland of the metal and engineering industries. The period of eighties marked the end of industrial era as a number of factories were going to wall one-by-one. The major manufacturing industries such as British Steel in Bilston where I had my first job, C.B.Smith, QualCast, GKN Sankey and many more closed down, creating mass unemployment, deprivation and industrial decay. The rate of unemployment in Wolverhampton disproportionately rose to 21% compared with 13% nationally. At least one third of the working age population was unemployed in certain parts of inner areas of the town such as Heath Town, Low Hill, St. Peter's, and Blaken-hall. The pressure of unemployment, poverty and deprivation generated a feeling of hopelessness, neglect and alienation amongst many leading to rejection and rebellion against society. Subsequently, all these circumstances gave rise to a dreadfully high crime rate, increased domestic violence, and broken marriages resulting in a high rate of divorce and child neglect.

Consequently, criminal activities were on the rise, and attacks on the elderly and vulnerable were headline news every day. There was one particular incident which touched the heart of every law-abiding resident of this town. An elderly woman of 86, living alone in her house, was badly beaten and robbed in broad daylight. Her badly bruised and blood stained face was printed on the front pages of local and national newspapers and shown on BBC Midlands Today. It was an extremely horrible and shamefully barbaric attack on one of our most vulnerable members of our society.

Many community organisations in the town held meetings

with the police and raised their concerns about law and order and the safety and security of the most vulnerable members of the society. I personally attended a couple of such meetings, listened to their concerns on safety particularly at night-time. The residents of Wolverhampton expected the Mayor of the town to raise the profile of those issues which most concerned the residents and to do something about the situation in the town.

In the circumstances, I felt obliged to do something to restore confidence in the residents of Wolverhampton and build public trust in police. I had several ideas mind such as raising public awareness, promoting joint efforts between neighbour-hood watch schemes and community policing and leading discussions between community leaders and David Ebb's, the Chief Superintendent of Police in the town. I organised two successful events, with the collaboration of police and other interested parties, to raise public awareness to combat criminal activities. One of the events, 'Tribute to victims of mugging', I organised in the Mayor's parlour and the second 'Home Safe Home' at the Grand Theatre, Wolverhampton. The local police provided me with a list of elderly victims of crime over the previous twelve months, and I sent them all an invitation. For the Tribute meeting the police, in civilian clothes, were on hand to provide transport to bring them to the parlour.

I am pleased to print details of the programmes, press coverage and some of the photos of the events. I start with the speech I made at the Grand Theatre:

> *"Ladies and gentlemen, brothers and sisters and distinguished guests,*
> *We gather here to launch 'HOME SAFE HOME' a crime prevention programme.*
> *The recent shameful events that have appeared in the*

On the front a group of elderly victims of crime, standing on the back from left to right are one of the police officers, the Lady Mayoress, Chief Superintendent Mr David Ebbs, myself and Cllr. Ray Swatman.

media have touched the minds of every civilized human being. One of the most worrying problems in modern society is the increase in crimes against our elderly. Very often, they feel isolated and vulnerable and in some cases, this can make their lives extremely miserable. It is a challenge to make society a safe place to live in for everyone. And the time is crying out for a positive approach that will allay their fears and make them feel more safe and secure.

A number of voluntary and community organisations throughout our town have embarked upon a projects and taken initiatives to combat crime in our society. I am extremely grateful to all those organisations for responding to my call for action against crime.

151

One of the best approaches to combat crime is by creating an atmosphere of awareness and education. The words may seem sluggish and slightly uninteresting but used in a proper way can be stimulating, instructive and entertaining. And tonight's event has been organised with that in mind. There is not any reason why you should not be entertained and learn something at the same time. The "Home Safe Home" Programme aims to achieve that balance and I sincerely hope that today will prove lots of fun and gives you an idea of how to make your home and yourself more secure. And none of us are too old to learn, as this evening will prove."

Mayor's tribute to mugging victims

The courage and bravery of nine elderly victims of vicious muggings has been marked with a civic reception by Wolverhampton's Mayor.

Councillor Bishan Dass yesterday invited the nine victims — most of them pensioners — to lunch in the Mayor's Parlour to publicly honour them.

It was part of the Mayor's campaign over attacks and to get the community to keep an eye on elderly neighbours.

Victims of some of the more horrific muggings had been selected to have lunch with the Mayor. Among them was widow Mrs Ivy Williams, who was pounced on and dragged along the road by her attacker just two days before her 80th birthday in February.

She is pictured shaking hands with the Mayor's wife, Ram Piara.

Mrs Williams, of Grimsby Estate,

She said she was walking along Mor-rdale Street, Wolverhampton, with her neighbour, Mrs Margaret Hall, aged 74, when they were pounced on by two teenage boys.

One grabbed Mrs Hall's bag but Mrs Williams refused to release hers and she was dragged along the ground. The attacker eventually fled empty-handed.

The Mayor and Mayoress, accompanied by council and police representatives, talked to the victims about their ordeals during the lunch.

Wolverhampton Council wish to thank the following
who have contributed to the event:

Birmingham Midshires Building Society
Wolverhampton Crime Prevention Panel
West Midlands Police
The Grand Theatre
Doug Parker
Central Youth Theatre
Wolverhampton Musical Comedy Group
Gardenians Marching Jazz Band
Community Transport
St. John's Ambulance
West Midlands Fire Prevention Team
Age Concern
Crypt-Victim Support Team
Spurgeons Group Work
Merridale Community Project
Bilston Congregational Church Centre
Connect Ltd.
Marks and Spencer PLC
Beatties
Sainsbury's
Yale Security Products Ltd.
British Home Stores

Crime Prevention Panel

HOME SAFE HOME

**Wednesday November 19th
at the
Grand Theatre
Wolverhampton**

WOLVERHAMPTON
COUNCIL Caring for you

The programme for the "Home Safe Home" event at the Grand Theatre in
Wolverhampton. It was a considerable success.

Programme of Events

2.00 p.m.	Welcoming address by The Worshipful the Mayor of Wolverhampton.
2.10 p.m.	'Crime and the Elderly' - Acting Chief Superintendent Phil Veaters, Home Office Crime Prevention Centre.
2.20 p.m.	'Knock, knock, who's there?' Central Youth Theatre.
2.45 p.m.	'A Guide to the best way to invest your savings.' Birmingham Midshires Building Society.
2.50 p.m.	Refreshments.
3.20 p.m.	Old Time Music Sing-Song, Wolverhampton Musical Comedy Group.
3.45 p.m.	Prize Draw by the Mayoress.
	Compere - Doug Parker, Comedian.

HOME SAFE HOME

HEATH TOWN SENIOR CITIZENS

As I mentioned earlier I attended approximately 2,600 engagements during my year of mayoralty. I hosted and organised some of these functions in the Mayor's Parlour and I encouraged as many individuals, community and residents organisations to visit the parlour. There are many people still who have never had the opportunity to look inside the parlour and have no idea about what actually takes place. For many of those that I did invite it was a fascinating experience and they were extremely happy and proud at the end of their visit. One such visit was from a group of senior citizens from Heath Town, and they were entertained for an afternoon tea in the Parlour. We combined it with a

The Heath Town Over 60s Club members who were one of the many groups to have been invited to the Mayor's Parlour.

short talk by the local police who were on hand to make the visitors aware of how to stay safe at home. They expressed their gratitude in the letter below.

MR. Albert Love. Secretary:
Heath Town Residents Assoc.
240 Charvil Rise
Heath Town.
Wolverhampton.
2/10/86:

Dear Councillor Dass,

I am writing to say what an honour it was for myself, and my fellow members whom you invited to meet yourself, and your wife. May I also express to you our sincere thanks, for a most interesting tour of the mayoral suite, and for a very enjoyable dinner as well. We all thank you very much for this nice gesture. We send you both our best wishes and good luck in your term of office as our mayor.

P.s. I would like to conclude by saying that you have earned this position for all the hard work you have done over the past years as councillor. you have helped us with many problems in Heath Town for which we are very grateful to you for and hope you will continue to in the future:

Once again good luck to you and your lady wife.

Yours Sincerely
Albert Love
Secretary

155

OFFICIAL OPENING OF THE WOLVERHAMPTON TRADE UNION EDUCATION AND INFORMATION CENTRE

"Ladies/Gentlemen,

It is with great pleasure I welcome you all to the official opening of the Wolverhampton Trade Union Education & Information Service. I am pleased to welcome our distinguished guest, Mr Norman Willis, the General Secretary of the National Trades Union Council, to Wolverhampton. It is a measure of the importance of this initiative that we are honoured by his presence .

Brothers and sisters, as a member of the Leisure Services Committee for the last four years, I am a part of the group to set up this centre. The Committee visited Birmingham and Coventry last year and looked at similar facilities there. The information and education regarding trades union affairs are vital not only for their trades union members but it is equally important for employers in order to improve labour relations.

I am proud to be able to participate in the launch of this exciting new joint venture. And I firmly believe that it will provide an essential and long awaited service for trade union members, employers and for the public in Wolverhampton and the surrounding areas.

And before handing over the platform to my colleague, Councillor Andrew Johnson the chair of the sub-committee, I have the great pleasure in introducing our other guests:-

Rt.Hon. Bob Edwards MP for the Wolverhampton South East constituency, Mr Jim Smith, chair of the West Midlands T.U.C. Education Advisory Committee, Councillor

Alan Garner, chair of the Polytechnic Governing Council, Mr Denis Turner, who is representing the board of governors of Bilston Community college, Mr Allan Gaunt, representing both education and trades unions in Wolverhampton.

A historic photograph of Norman Willis, General Secretary of the YUC together with other trades union leaders at the Mayor's Parlour.

I had the pleasure of meeting and greeting both the past and present General Secretaries of the Trade Union Council, Mr Jack Jones and Mr Norman Willis. I had the privilege and pride to receive these two very distinguished leaders of the national Trades Union Council at the Mayor's Parlour. I found Mr Willis most sociable and very closely interested in the interests of working class people.

SOROPTIMISTS, WOLVERHAMPTON
21st November 1986

"Brothers/sisters,
I have a great pleasure in responding to the toast.
It is important to know now that the town had a wide range
of organisations representing many different interests. We
have a veritable mixture of commercial and industrial
businesses, small and large, and there are a large number of
voluntary community and statutory organisations as well.
And all of them together are providing a very valuable net-
work of public services, working for most common interests
to the benefit of the people of this town.
A great deal of this success has been achieved through their
efforts to change the image and infrastructure of the town
and still there lots, lots more to achieve. The most difficult
issue of the day, unfortunately happens to be the recession,
which has had a drastic effect on our economic and
industrial recovery. Since 1979 we have lost almost 1,100
manufacturing jobs in the metal industry, and this in turn
has affected recovery in the service industries.
Consequently, the multiple of deprivation is having a deep
effect on family and social life of the people of our town.
Unfortunately, the town has suffered a disproportionately
high percentage of unemployment and deprivation.
Unemployment is the major evil amongst us. Ten years ago,
2500 unemployed in our town would have been unbeliev-
able, but now a reality.
The lack of investment in both the public and private sectors
has seriously affected confidence in the industry and further
added to the deprivation and created problems which we

will have to face in the future. The local authority is under increased pressure to maintain services in the face of reduced resources. Drastic reductions in government grant funding is making it extremely difficult to meet the demand whilst still maintaining the same level of services. The real effect on life is more than it appears on the surface with 37,000 people on housing benefit, 4,000 on job seekers allowance. Your local council is trying its best to provide every possible help and support to industry in job creation programmes and undertaking initiatives designed to provide opportunities for employment.

Brothers and sisters, despite all the difficulties and problems of recession and deprivation I have mentioned, we have common interests and goals for the good of all the people of the town."

160

WOLVERHAMPTON JUDO CLUB RECEPTION

Wolverhampton has a long history of producing world class sports talent—including in judo. Wolverhampton Judo Club was started at Heath Town Baths on Tudor Road as early as the 1980s and in a very short time became a beacon of national excellence, and gained international recognition. The Wolverhampton team won a number of national competitions and eventually trained for international contests. They came second in the European championship in 1986 and they gained huge national popularity and the town was extremely proud of them.

On behalf of the people of Wolverhampton, I was delighted to organize a reception on 22nd November for the team. A presentation was organised at the Mander Centre prior to a reception in the Mayor's Parlour. A large crowd gathered around the stage at the Mander Centre and Councillor Arthur Stevenson, chair of the Leisure Services Committee, started the proceedings. He welcomed everyone, said few words, and invited me to speak:

> *"Dear Brothers/Sisters,*
> *Wolverhampton is proud to acknowledge some of the special sports personalities from the town and it gives me great pleasure to make these special presentations to them.*
> *Firstly, our young sports people who represented us at the Special Olympics at Brighton earlier this year.*
> *Secondly our splendid Judo squad who are unable to be here today because they are busy working on our behalf to represent Wolverhampton in the finals of the European Championship in France next weekend."*

In fact the Judo team came second in the European

Wolverhampton's Judo-team receive medals of thanks from the Mayor, Councillor Bishan Dass.

Judo Team Gets Big Thanks

A second place in Europe doesn't stop Wolverhampton's Judo team from being top in the town.

The squad only won silver medals in the European Club Team Championships but Wolverhampton Council gave them a gold for their achievements.

The eight man squad were narrowly defeated in the final, last November, but in the eyes of their supporters they were winners.

It was the first time they entered the contest but they were only able to do so thanks to financial help from the council.

Mayor, councillor Bishan Dass, pation possible. Without their help and that of the council we would never have taken part''.

The Wolverhampton Judo Club plans to enter the contest again later this year. It currently trains weekday evenings at Graisley Recreation Centre and Heath Town Swimming Baths.

(pictured), presented the Judo team with medals of thanks at a special ceremony and said he hopes to see them go one better next time.

Squad coach, Mac Abbotts said: "We would like to thank all the people of Wolverhampton who made our partici-

Championship, narrowly missing out on the Gold Medal. However, on their return to Wolverhampton a special presentation when each member of the squad was given a special commemorative medal.

DEALING WITH CASE WORK

I was very passionate about casework from the very begin-ning—indeed perhaps that is what brought me into public life. I inherited the quality to provide help and support to others in need from my family in childhood . This was, I feel, my life long mission and has remained a source of happiness and strength throughout my life. I have found that it inspires me, makes me enthusiastic, full of strength and provides me a great deal of inner satisfaction. As I have mentioned earlier that I used to be readily available and willing to help people in need irrespective of where they come from and who they are. There were high expectations of me during my year of mayoralty particularly by people from the ethnic minority communities. Often people used to come, with-out making an appointment, to see me at the Parlour asking for help and support and I would always find time from my busy schedule to listen to them.

I would like to mention here one particular case of a problem of immigration, involving a British born woman called Sarbjeet Kaur Chander who was married to an illegal immigrant called Som Raj. They had two children but he was facing deportation orders to leave the country (although there was an appeal pending in the high court against the order). This case attracted nationwide publicity in the media and on TV. Mrs Chander wrote a letter to me, requesting my help and support regarding the deportation orders against her husband. Already formed was a campaign committee comprising several individuals, representatives of local organisations together with support from some Members of Parliament. The members of the campaign committee, along with Mrs Chander and her husband ,came to see me at the Parlour and after listening her case; I too pledged my support. I wrote letters of support to Her

Majesty the Queen, David Waddington (the Minister for Immigration) and Bob Edwards, the local Member of Parliament. I urged them to reconsider the case of Mr Raj with a view to granting him leave to stay due to the fact that he was married to a British born girl and they had a young family. At the same time I raised some other issues concerning the plight of newly arrived black migrants at Heathrow Airport and the fact that a large number of them were being routinely detained at the Queen's Building.

I have included copies of some of the letters I wrote and the replies that I received and one of the many press cuttings that accompanied the story.

The Rt. Hon. Mayor
Bishan Dass.
Civic Centre
Wolverhampton.

10.6.86.

Rt. Hon. Bishan Dass.

I beg to inform you that The Home Office is trying to deport my husband to India. We are happily married with two young Children aged 21 Months and 10 Months. My husband's deportation will mean the breaking up of a happy married family which is not justice.

We would be much obliged to your honour if you could support us and have a mercy to save this family from great deal of sufferings and ask the Home Secretary to let my husband stay with his family.

Thank you.

Yours Sincerely
S. K. Chander.
Our Home Office Ref. R220331

The original letter from Mrs Chander requesting that I support the case of her husband who was due to be deported as an illegal immigrant.

MAYOR'S PARLOUR
CIVIC CENTRE
ST PETER'S SQUARE
WOLVERHAMPTON
WVI IRG

TELEPHONE Nº 27011

13th August 1986

Dear Private Secretary,

I am writing to you to express my grave concern with regard to the threatened deportation of Mr Som Raj

In April, 1983, Mr Raj came as a visitor for six months to see his sister, who was unwell, and her family in Wolverhampton.

During this time he met Sarjeet Kaur Chander, whom he married on 22 August, 1983, and they set up home in Wolverhampton. In September he applied for leave to stay in the United Kingdom as the husband of a British wife — (Sarjeet was born and brought up here).

The Immigration Authorities refused him leave to stay on the ground that they were of the opinion that the primary purpose of marriage was to gain settlement in this country.

Mr Raj appealed against this decision to the Home Office Adjudicator. In September, 1984, the Adjudicator allowed his appeal by stating inter alia "I am bound to find a valid marriage between the parties ... and the parties have been living together permanently ... I allow this appeal and I direct that entry clearance be granted to the appellant".

The Home Office, however, was not satisfied with this direction and appealed to the Immigration Appeals Tribunal. In April, 1985, the Tribunal reversed the Adjudicator's direction and, since then, the threat of deportation has hung over Som Raj. .

Mr Raj has a secure and successful job as a photographer in the town. He and his wife Sarjeet now have two young daughters Zeklina (20 months) and Anglika (9 months). They enjoy a very happy family life in the Parkfields area of Wolverhampton and his deportation would mean the break-up of a stable and happily settled family with the consequent heartache and difficulties for his wife and children.

The case against Som Raj's deportation is a just one. I appeal to you on humanitarian and compassionate grounds and urge that Mr Raj's case be reviewed immediately with a view to allowing him to stay, thus ending the uncertainty and unhappiness of the family.

I would like to take this opportunity to raise two further issues that are causing considerable concern to many of the citizens of Wolverhampton and, in particular, those who have had to deal with the Immigration Services.

Police cells are frequently used to detain visitors - 52 were held during July and, in recent weeks, up to 30 passengers were forced to spend the night on the floor of the immigration section at Heathrow Airport owing to the lack of adequate staffing and facilities. As a result of being detained under such dreadful conditions and through no fault of their own, the good name of the Queen's Building is now being called the 'Black Detention Centre'. I understand that individuals of all ages, which includes mothers, very young children and old-age pensioners, have been subjected to such inhuman treatment.

Secondly, the EEC ruling on the question of the discriminatory effect of the immigration rules concerning the entry of husbands and fiances, has meant that these rules are now equally bad for both men and women.

Not only was the legislation changed to demand that men too must satisfy the 'primary purpose of marriage' test but it must now also be shown that both men and women can maintain themselves in this country. I feel that this additional requirement may lead to even further delays and families who suffer from being divided will continue to do so.

The black community and especially the Asian community face particular difficulty in satisfying these requirements due to the long standing tradition of arranged marriages and it is estimated that over 90% of cases are being refused entry and, consequently, a legitimate right of many citizens of this country wanting to bring their life partner is being denied simply on grounds of suspicion.

The matters I have raised are causing a great deal of concern to me and damage to harmonious Race Relations in Wolverhampton. I trust you will give them your urgent attention and look forward to their early resolution in a manner that is considered just by all.

Yours sincerely,

From: Bob Edwards MP

HOUSE OF COMMONS
LONDON SWIA OAA

4th September 1986

Dear Councillor Dass,

As you know, your letter to HM The Queen was
passed to me via the Prime Minister's Office and I have
now forwarded it to the Minister concerned. I will let
you know as soon as I receive his reply.

Sincerely yours,

Bob Edwards

Cllr Bishan Dass
Mayor of Wolverhampton

10 DOWNING STREET
LONDON SWIA 2AA

18 August 1986

Dear Sir

I am writing to thank you for
your recent letter which is receiving
attention.

Yours faithfully

Betty Cann

Mayor of Wolverhampton
(Councillor B Dass)
Mayor's Parlour
Civic Centre
St Peter's Square
WOLVERHAMPTON
WV1 1RG

168

QUEEN ANNE'S GATE LONDON SW1H 9AT

Our ref: P220331/26(S)

Thank you for your letter of 13 August which as you know Her Majesty The Queen's Private Secretary has forwarded me for reply, about Mr Som Raj, a citizen of India, who has been refused leave to remain in the United Kingdom as the husband of a woman settled here.

Mr Raj's circumstances have been considered on a number of occasions as several Members of Parliament and others have made representations on his behalf. It is true that an independent adjudicator accepted that a valid marriage had taken place and that the couple intended to live togehter. He went on, however, to find that the primary purpose of the marriage was to obtain settlement and only allowed the appeal because of the precedent decisions of the Tribunal which then applied. Subsequently, the Tribunal reversed its earlier decisions on the interpretations of the "primary purpose" rule and this was confirmed in the High Court in the case of Vinod Bhatia, and more recently in the case of Arun Kumar. Consequently we thought it right to seek leave to appeal to the Tribunal in the case of Mr Raj and, as you know, the Tribunal reversed the adjudicator's determination and upheld the original refusal.

Both I and Mr Waddington, the Minister of State responsible for immigration matters, have carefully reviewed the case again, in the light of the various representations that have been received, including you own, but we are not prepared to overturn the decision which has been upheld by the Tribunal. Mr Raj will shortly be invited to put forward any new mitigating factors which he would like to be considered before a decision whether or not to deport him is finally taken.

On a more general note, you have referred to the current provisions for the admission of spouses and fiance(e)s and in particular the primary purpose test. As you know, changes were made to the provisions in the Immigration Rules providing for the admission of men and women on the basis of marriage to comply with the judgement last year of the European Court of Human Rights. The Government took the view then that it would be right to extend the right to bring in a husband or male fiance to women who were settled but not British citizens. You may like to know that as a result of this change to the Rules we expect that the numbers accepted for settlement each year are likely to rise by about 2,000 worldwide, including some six hundred from the Indian sub-continent.

/There

MAYOR'S PARLOUR
0 5 JAN 1987
RECEIVED

Councillor B Dass

169

There was nothing in the European Court's judgement which called into question the requirements in the Rules which husbands must satisfy to qualify for admission. On the contrary, the legitimacy of the objective in the Rules was endorsed by the Court. The Government took the view that it was entirely reasonable if we were to comply with the principle of the judgement while maintaining strict immigration control that the marriage tests applying to the admission of husbands should be retained and extended to apply on the same basis to the admission of wives.

You quote a figure of over 90% of cases being refused entry. I can assure you that this figure is incorrect: in 1985 about 35% of all decided applications from husbands and fiancés in the Indian sub-continent were refused solely because the applicants failed the primary purpose test.

The maintenance and accommodation requirements which must be met by all spouses and fiance(e)s (except wives benefiting from the statutory protection afforded by section 1(5) of the Immigration Act 1971) are designed to prevent the admission of those who have no realistic prospects of supporting themselves without recourse to public funds. At a time of restraint on public expenditure and strain on our existing resources, the Government felt that it was right to extend and strengthen the existing tests. The tests are not however a device to keep those who qualify out. In the case of a spouse or fiance(e) what the applicant, has to do is to satisfy the entry clearance officer that adequate maintenance and accommodation will be available. The test will not hinder the admission of applicants who have qualifications or skills that will ensure they can make a positive contribution to our society.

I have also noted your concern about the number of passengers detained by the Immigration Service at Heathrow Airport. I should explain that the power to detain a passenger required to submit to further examination or refused entry is used sparingly, but you will appreciate that it is the immigration officer who is required, in the first instance, to decide whether or not that person is likely to comply with the conditions of temporary admission. The need for detention is reviewed locally by the port inspector and is maintained only where it is the view of the officers concerned that the risk of a passenger failing to comply with the conditions of temporary admission is unacceptably high. I am conscious of the pressures on the Immigration Service and the lack of suitable detention accommodation as a result of the large increase in the number of passengers arriving at Heathrow Airport in recent months. I would wish to assure you however that we are looking at ways of improving immigration detention facilities.

Not exactly the answer we were hoping for.

WOLVERHAMPTON CHRONICLE, FRIDAY, AUGUST 22, 1986 — Page

MAYOR WRITES TO THE QUEEN IN BID TO STOP DEPORTATION

LET HIM STAY

Som Raj

REPORT BY MIKE WILLIAMS

SOM Raj is an ordinary family man who came to this country in 1983 to visit his poorly sister in Wolverhampton, and shortly afterwards met and married his wife Sarjeet.

... In the town, and the occasional successful job as a photographer ... daughters Zealina, aged 20 months, and nine-month-old ...

But the story of an ordinary family man ends there. Because Som Raj has the threat of deportation hanging over his head. And many thousands have the disastrous news that he will be sent packing back to India and he and his family might be separated forever.

For exactly a comfortable way to live, although he has had strong support from his church, community, political and cultural organisations, and the latest appeal, the Mayor of Wolverhampton, Councillor Bashan Dass, who has joined a letter to the Queen for Mr Raj to stay in Britain ... with the appeal. "I am writing to express my grave concern over this," says Bashan Dass in the letter.

"In April 1983 Mr Raj came as a visitor for six months to see his sister, who was unwell, and her family in Wolverhampton. Around this time he met Sarjeet Kaur Chandan, who he married on April 22, 1983, and they set up home in Wolverhampton.

Appeal against decision

"In September he applied for leave to stay in the UK as the husband of a British wife (Sarjeet, now here and brought up ...) ... The immigration authorities refused him leave to stay ... this. The marriage was not the primary purpose of marriage was to settle in this country ...

"Mr Raj appealed against this decision to the Home Office ... appeal hearing in September 1984 the adjudicator allowed the appeal by stating ... the parties had a valid marriage between the parties ... and the parties have been living together permanently ... I allow this appeal, and I direct that entry clearance be granted to the appellant ...

"The Home Office, however, not satisfied with this direction and appealed to the Immigration Appeals Tribunal. In April 1985 the tribunal reversed the adjudicator's direction ... and the threat of deportation has hung over Som Raj.

Mr Raj is a secure and successful job as a photographer in the town. He and his wife, Sarjeet, now have two young children, Zealina ... and ... They enjoy a very happy family life in this part of ... Wolverhampton and this deportation would mean the break-up ... and happily settled family with the consequent ... heartache and hardship to his wife and children.

Appeal to you on humanitarian and compassionate grounds and urges that Mr Raj's case be reviewed immediately ... and urges that Mr Raj's case be reviewed immediately with a ... people harmless to sleep on the floor, thus ending the uncertainty and unhappiness of the family.

Mr Dass's letter continues by calling attention to the issue of visitors to this country being detained at Heathrow Airport, which has inadequate facilities for detentions and leads to people harmless to sleep on the floor.

He also highlights the EEC ruling on the question of the entry of husbands and fiancées, which means these rules are now equally bad for both men and women.

The letter says that legislation has been changed to demand that men too must satisfy the 'primary purpose of marriage' test, but it must now also be shown that both men and women can remain in themselves in this country.

He says: "I fear that this additional requirement may lead to even further delays and families who suffer from being ..."

Copies of the letter have been sent to Prime Minister Margaret Thatcher, Neil Kinnock, Home Office Minister David Waddington, Gerald Kaufman, and also to local MPs Mrs Kaur has absolute faith in the campaign, and says their ... say: "I am tremendous support, including that of 19 MPs. She ... we also had tremendous support, because of the ... support, plus the fact that we are British born, and British is ...

Mr Dass continues: "Of course we met any prejudice in the case of Mr Raj, saying, "Of course we met any prejudice in the ... great majority of this type of case are immigrants, because the ... side to go to the tribunal, which does not act for any party alone.

"We have the right to do this as Mr Raj would have done if the appeal had gone against him.

"We wanted the tribunal's opinion on the adjudicator's decision.

"And the tribunal's determination was that Mr Raj had entered into the marriage primarily for a British settlement in the UK, and therefore allowed our appeal.

"Despite the immediate threat of imminent deportation, the struggle goes on for the family and the campaign supporters.

There are no immediate plans for the future, only the continuation of a fight in which Mr Raj is convinced he will win and justice will, in the end, be done.

BISHAN DASS — His Majesty

171

BIRMINGHAM CITY 1992 OLYMPIC BID

During 1986 the City of Birmingham bid for the 1992 Olympic Games. They had all-round support from central government, all seven West Midlands councils and the whole community West Midlands behind them. The City Council prepared an excellent bid and hopes were high for success. There was great enthusiasm and excitement all over the region and people were making offers of every possible financial and moral support and many community and voluntary organisations held fundraising activities. All the seven West Midlands councils made financial contributions towards preparing the bid and the whole area was expecting to gain a great deal from the Olympics taking place in Birmingham.

Wolverhampton was the designated venue for the shooting competition (to be held at Aldersley Stadium) as we had superb facilities that were much better than other councils in West Midlands. A huge publicity campaign in the local and national media raised the profile of the whole Midland area and a range of memorabilia such as badges, key rings, pens, ties and clips depicting the Olympic 1992 logo were produced to add to the publicity campaign. I was given a number of such items to give away to many visitors to the Parlour. Unfortunately, the bid was to prove unsuccessful due to combination of several factors , including strained relations with Middle East countries due to the USA bombing Libya, British government support for the South African claim to participate in the Olympics as unprecedented nationwide racial tension particularly riots in Birmingham's Handsworth district. Wolverhampton Council contributed £150,000 towards the preparation of the bid. I had the honour of presenting the cheque to Mr Taylor of Birmingham City Council.

Presenting the cheque for £150,000 towards the cost of the bid for Birmingham to be awarded the 1992 Olympic Games.

WOLVERHAMPTON MULTI-HANDICAP GROUP
10th September 1986

"Mr Chairman, Ladies and Gentlemen,
Thank you for your invitation to the official opening of the
Centre. It is a great privilege indeed because caring and look-
ing after those who are in an unfortunate situation of not
being able to look after themselves is a most humane task.
It is difficult to assess and describe the problems and pressure
upon a family with a child born with multiple disabilities.

It is extremely hard work and a challenge to the whole family. A little help and support to look after a handicapped person is a great relief to all involved.

I commend all the efforts and very hard work that the Wolverhampton Multi-Handicap Group has put into organising and establishing a centre here in the town. The Relief Care scheme they have now set up will take care of handicapped persons in their homes and a significant number of families will benefit from it.

Wolverhampton Multi-Handicap Group has taken on the challenge and it is our moral responsibility to give them the best of our support and encouragement.

I wish the Centre every success for their good cause and it is with much pleasure that I now declare the premises open.

FESTIVAL OF LANGUAGES
COLTON HILL COMPHREHENSIVE SCHOOL
October 1986

"Ladies , gentlemen and children,
I am pleased to open this Festival of Languages. It is the first one to be held here in Wolverhampton and I hope it will not be the last. Wolverhampton is now a multi-cultural and multi-racial society and our town is an area rich in many languages from many different cultures. I am therefore sure all of us will learn something from this festival.
We all know the importance of languages in modern society. It helps us to communicate with people from many different ethnic backgrounds. We can learn and understand each other and resolve many misunderstandings amongst us. The diversity of culture is our strength and many different languages and cultures which exist side-by-side should not prove to be barrier. Instead it should provide a strong bond which can bring us closer to each other.
Many young people from our schools will be demonstrating various language skills such as Hindi, Punjabi, Urdu, Polish, French and German etc. I hope I will be able to add to the Festival as I can speak at least four languages.
I have been told that for those who are interested, there will be twenty minute language lessons for beginners held every week during the daytime. Although we will be seeing and hearing young people demonstrating the languages through-out the day, I would like to remind those of you who slightly older, that the languages are not just for the young. It's never too late to learn a language and once you overcome the first few hurdles it will become very enjoyable. You will also find yourself getting interested in the people who speak

176

the language and you will want to know more about their culture and customs.

Therefore languages can provide a bridge between different people and their cultures. It is a most useful bridge over which we should all want to cross and I hope many of you will take the first step onto that bridge today. I am aware that there is an excellent language department at this school and at many others and I urge you all to make use of the   facilities available. I will be interested to come back here in a year's time and hear you all speaking different languages. And now I will speak few minutes in Hindi and Punjabi and translate it in English. I sincerely hope that you will fully enjoy it.

Thank you for you patience for listening to me."

OPENING OF ABBEYFIELD HOUSE, TETTENHALL
12th July 1986

The opening of Abbeyfield House was another interesting civic duty at which I had the honour of cutting the ribbon to declare the house open. The opening of Abbyfield House was preceded by a nice lunch at St. Michael's Parish Church on Tettenhall Road. Mr Peter Howell William, the national chair of the Abbeyfield Society spoke about Abbeyfield activities all over the country. He said that they now had over 1000 houses managed by 600 societies and run by over 900 volunteers. He further said that the society had taken its place at the forefront of a growing national movement and was beginning to have international recognition. There were at least 70 people present including a number of VIPs like Nick Budgen MP, Guy Smith, Ron Rock, Bill Boyd and local councillor John Davis.
I was then asked to respond to Mr William's address:

"Mr Chairman, Honourable Member of Parliament and guests,
First of all, I would like to thank the Society for inviting me and the Mayoress to this very special occasion of the opening of Abbeyfields House and treating us to a very delicious lunch. And on behalf of the local authority, I welcome you all to our great town Wolverhampton.
Furthermore, I would like to thank Abbeyfields for selecting Wolverhampton to invest in through providing an excellent facility for our elderly. We have over 2,500 elderly people on our waiting list but due to shortage of resources, we are unable to their cater for all their needs.

The accommodation and facilities at Abbeyfields House are of a very high standard and I hope they will provide services to the elderly for many years to come.
Once again, on behalf of the council, I am grateful to you and your organisation for providing excellent accommodation of a very high standard.

Return to Abbeyfield

The charming and very comfortable Abbeyfield House in Church Hill Road has been open for some months now providing a home within a home for the retired residents.

Saturday July 12th was the official opening day by Bishan Dass, the town's Mayor accompanied by his wife. The occasion was preceded by an excellent lunch in the Parish Hall after which the many guests and officials of Abbeyfield walked across the Worgs Road to Church Hill Road full of good food and bonhomie. The sun shone warmly but intermittently, and when the guests walked around the house and grounds, admiring its many noble and delightful features, our photographer was trying to find a good position for an interesting photograph.

At 3.00pm the group of around sixty people including such notables as Tom Rock, Bill Boyd, Guy Smith, Nick Budgen and Councillor John Davis assembled before the front door to watch Bishan Dass cut the ribbon.

Speaking without notes the Mayor said he had been impressed by Abbeyfield and admired its concept. He spoke warmly of the benefits of providing this type of accommodation for the elderly. The local authority has 2,500 people on its list for special accommodation he said but does not have the resources to meet their need. Abbeyfield and organisations like it reduce the strain on the community's conscience and the Authority's finances.

We were particulary impressed by the impeccable timing of Trevor Roberts the 'Select' magazine photographer who arrived after Councillor Dass began his speech, and about 2 minutes before the tape was cut. Bishan Dass is an experienced speaker and we have wondered if he and Trevor had arranged together that the speech should not end until he had arrived to take a 'quality' picture.

It all worked out well anyway. The tape parted, cameras clicked, flowers were presented to the Mayoress, and everyone applauded. It had been a thoroughly enjoyable afternoon.

SCHOOL VISITS

I visited many primary and secondary schools and received children at the Parlour during my year of Mayoralty. The motive behind the visits to schools was educational and I am sure that many children benefited from them. I received a group of children from Brickkiln School, and more than twenty children wrote most interesting and nice letters about their experience of a visit to the Mayor's Parlour. It is not possible to print here all the letters so I have chosen a few that, I think, are typical examples:

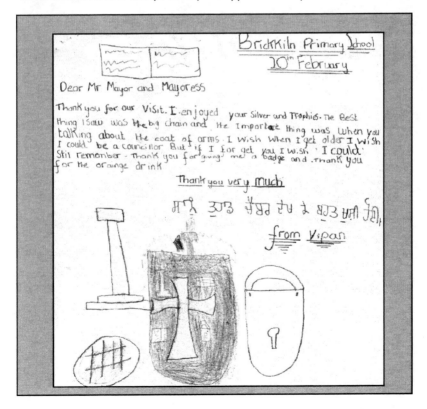

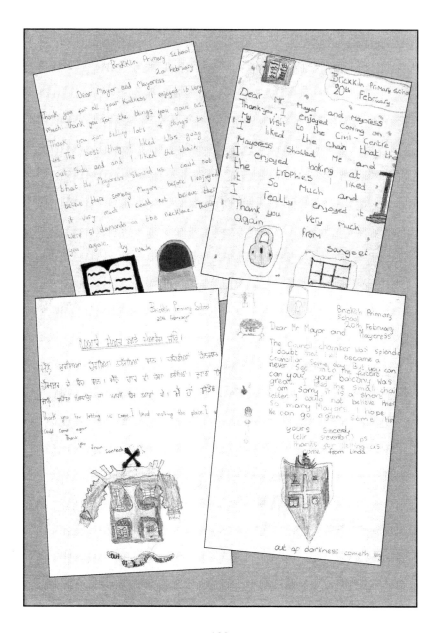

A VISIT TO NANTWICH
27th August 1986

I have mentioned previously that I had invitations from all over the country from Scotland to Yorkshire, Bedford, Cheshire, the Midlands and London. One of those invitations came from the Badhan family who invited me and the Mayoress to visit them at their supermarket in Nantwich in Cheshire. He and his wife came around one day to see me at the Mayor's Parlour in Wolverhampton. There was a full council meeting on that day and they sat in the public gallery until the meeting finished. It was a surprise visit and they were pleased to see me after the meeting. I greeted them in the Parlour for a cup of tea. They said it would be a great honour if we visited them at their supermarket in Cheshire. The Badhan family was originally from Wolverhampton and had strong connections with our town, and Mr Badhan had many friends and relatives still living here in Wolverhampton. I was obliged to accept his kind invitation and promised to visit them sometime during the year.

The Mayoress and I travelled up to Nantwich in August of that year. When we arrived the local press and a few other people had gathered waiting to greet us, and we had a warm welcome from the Badhan family and local residents. The Mayor of Nantwich was unable to attend due to a pre-booked prior engagement but did send a message of goodwill and best wishes to Mr Badhan and his family. We had a tour of their store and then we were invited for lunch with the family, friends and other guests. It was a most enjoyable visit and everyone was pleased to see us.

society. The Rt. Hon. Lord Scarman conducted an inquiry into the recent disturbances up and down the country and he summed up his findings as follows:-

Young people hanging around in the street all day with nothing to do and nowhere to go get together in groups and the 'successful' criminal has a story to tell. And one evil has bred another and as unemployment has grown in both elder and younger generations, crime has become more commonplace and more acceptable.

There is no present end in sight to this vicious circle. These circumstances have become a real threat to law and order and peace in society. If we want peace in society, we must pay the price. The role of law and order is to provide justice and equality of opportunity to all – and the real solution does not lie in oppressive measures as more oppression generates more agitation and violence.

A real solution, of course, depends upon a successful outcome of our current economic problems, and renewed initiatives. We must concentrate our efforts in attacking those conditions that generate despair and violence, create poverty and frustrations, divide society into haves and have nots.

Therefore, brothers and sisters, we must create an atmosphere of mutual understanding and sense of unity amongst us all in order to make a joint effort to overcome evils in society and work to create a peaceful society.

Last but not the least I would like to thanks sincerely for inviting me and providing with an opportunity to speak to the congregation."

NEW YEAR'S MESSAGE

It is customary for the mayor of the town to send a message of best wishes to the residents of the town as we enter each new year. In my New Year message, I touched upon some of my personal problems of hardship and racial prejudice in the early days of my life here in England. I touched upon issues such as economic deprivation, hardship, poverty and high unemployment faced by people of Wolverhampton. In return, I had several messages of appreciation, compliments, goodwill and best wishes from many townspeople. As you can see the local paper covered it in full:

A VISIT TO BEDFORD
18th January 1987

The Dr B.R. Ambedkar Mission Society of Bedford invited me to speak at their AGM and public meeting in early January 1987. I referred in my Mayor Making speech to Dr B.R. Ambedkar and his humanitarian mission for the welfare of downtrodden people in India and so I was particularly pleased to accept this invitation from the organisation working in the UK according to the life and mission of Dr.Ambedkar. The Society organised this event to take place in a large hall and widely publicised it, the result of which was that it attracted an audience of more than six hundred people. There were people from many different community organisations, churches, temples, local councillors, a Member of Parliament, and other VIPs, many of whom participated in the programme.

I was pleased to know that many of them came to see and listen to the very first Mayor of Indian origin. The Mayor of Bedford was informed about my visit, and he kindly invited me to his parlour for a cup of tea before going to the conference hall itself. Members of the Dr B.R. Ambedkar Mission Society accompanied me to the Mayor's office where enjoyed a very warm welcome. He was please to receive us and as a matter of respect presented me with an interesting memorandum of declaration duly signed by him. At the end of my speech at the conference people from the audience asked me few questions, and I was pleased to answer them, I hope to their satisfaction. After the programme had finished I met a large number of people, shook hands and many of them wish to have photos with me and the Mayoress. My speech is shown opposite.

"Brothers and Sisters,

I am honoured to be invited and to speak at this programme. I am grateful to the Dr. B.R. Ambedkar International Mission Society of Bedford for inviting me to attend and speak to the audience. The Mayor of Bedford kindly invited me to his parlour, itself a great honour, and I was pleased to make a short visit to see him before coming to this programme. I am grateful for his warm welcome and hospitality. I am pleased to know that the Ambedkar International Mission Society is working hard to promote the mission of Dr B.R. Ambedkar.

I am proud to be associated with and to have worked for Baba Sahib's mission over the past many years. In fact, the mission of Dr B.R. Ambedkar has hugely inspired my whole life. Often people asked me the reasons for being an Ambedkarite and my answer always is that when a person has been a victim of caste-based hatred and had suffered racial prejudice for his whole life it is natural for them to become a dedicated Ambedkarite.

And many of you would like to know what Ambedkarism is?

Ambedkarism is a simple but very difficult way of life. It stands on the four fundamental principles of equality, liberty, justice and peace, those attributes that are most essential for decent human life and modern civilised society. This mission is universal and it is not a monopoly of any caste, creed or religion; neither does it belong to a particular race or nationality. That is why when I took the office of mayoralty in May last year I made a pledge to devote my year in this office to promote this holy mission. I adopted 'EQUALITY, LIBERTY, JUSTICE and PEACE' as the main theme.

*British society over the past years has gradually trans-
formed from monolithic to pluralistic and now we are
living in a multi-cultural and multi-racial society. To
promote the theme of equality, liberty, justice and peace is
essential and badly needed in such a diverse society. To
establish a peaceful, happy and civilised society you have
to pay the price in terms of equality, liberty and justice.*

*I would like to mention here two particular issues that this
audience may be interested in for which there is cause for
concern.*

*Firstly, the whole subject of Immigration and Nationality
has caused a great deal of damage to harmonious
relations and created mistrust and ill feeling amongst
both the ethnic minorities and the indigenous society. The
1980 Immigration and Nationality Act introduced five
different categories of immigrants who can qualify to
come to this country. There is no doubt that it has
strengthened racial prejudice against people from black
and Asian countries.*

*Secondly, the recent move to introduce and tighten the
visa system for fiancées and visitors from five particular
countries has deepened wounds and caused further
damage to harmonious community relations.*

*Furthermore, the ever-increasing unemployment and
deprivation has not only divided the community but also
created north-south divide in the country. The whole
nation is now going through an extremely difficult period.
We are now faced with long lasting unemployment, a
decline in production industry and a poor environment
leading to poverty affecting family life and the social
fabric of our society. The problem is more serious in the
ethnic minorities, particularly for youngsters as they are*

the last to get employment opportunities. Consequently the poor living conditions are resulting in hopelessness, neglect and rejection amongst youngsters, adding fuel to rebellion against society. Very recently, we have experienced with concern the results of such feelings on our streets in many towns and cities up and down the country.

The Rt. Hon. Lord Scarman who conducted the inquiry into those recent disturbances summed up the solution to such problems. He said that the only genuine long-range solution to what had happened lies in an attack mounted at every level upon those conditions that breed despair and violence. Therefore, it is time for us to devote our efforts and energy to make sure policies and resources are geared and deployed to eliminate prejudice and discrimination in our society. And let us make sure that opportunities are available for all to progress in life. In addition, let us make sure we create a society of caring and sharing. We must make sure that we create an atmosphere of mutual understanding, tolerance and unity amongst all.

With these words, I wish you all my best wishes and thanks for coming along, and once again, I thank the committee for inviting the Mayoress and me and for providing us with such excellent hospitality."

The presentation certificate given to me by the Mayor of Bedford on the occasion of my visit to the Dr B.R. Ambedkar International Mission Society's conference.

A cutting from one of the Indian newspapers that reported on my visit to Bedford for the Dr B.R. Ambedkar International Mission Society's conference

LIGHTHOUSE MEDIA CENTRE
16th March 1987

The Lighthouse Media Centre was originally established at Wolverhampton Art Gallery in Lichfield Street, Wolverhampton and later moved just around the corner to the Chubb Building. As a member and vice chair of the Leisure Services Committee, I supported the inception of this project and subsequently I was invited to perform the opening ceremony, which I was delighted to do.

The Centre was part of an expansion programme for the Wolverhampton Art Gallery and was designed to revitalise the town centre. The focus was to make it attractive to students from the local polytechnic and encourage then to establish their own business as well as helping local industry with modern technology. The aim of the Centre was to provide a popular setting to create a venue for the enjoyment and understanding of modern media as a part of everyday life. It enabled greater emphasis to be placed on the importance of future contributions to the economic, cultural and social wellbeing of the area from the artistic and media worlds.. The first stage of this was the installation of very sophisticated equipment and a video production suite with advanced computer graphics and a studio cinema was. The Lighthouse was equipped to provide seasons of films, courses on film-making, training and exhibitions as well as enhancing the opportunities for the participation in all the skills such as video, photography and sound that are necessary in making a valuable contribution to public entertainment.

> "Thank you and can I say how delighted I am to see everyone here on this occasion.
> It gives me particular pleasure that I should have the

opportunity in my year of office to open a project which is unique, not just in Wolverhampton but in the West Midlands. This project is aimed at all sections of the community and will foster better community relations in the town, and in particular I hope that it will be of benefit to young people.

I believe it is important, especially at the current time, not to lose sight of the fact that this town has much to be proud of and much that has been achieved in recent years. Projects such as this play a small but important part in bringing life and activity into the town centre and building upon the talents and skills of Wolver-hampton people.

Much has already been achieved here—the project has sophisticated video production equipment and the studio theatre, in which you are now sitting, is fully operational. It is now in a position to present a full programme of courses, training, educational activities, film seasons and special events. Such activities will contribute to the cultural and social life of Wolver-hampton.

Last, but by no means least, can I thank the people in the room who represent other funding agencies, which in coming together with us have made this project possible. I understand that this is only the starting point and that there are many ambitious plans for the future. We are all aware of the pressures on resources faced by local authorities at this point in time but nevertheless I am sure you will all join me in wishing the project well. It gives me great pleasure to declare the lighthouse Media Centre open."

Trying out some of the sophisticated film and video equipment at the newly opened Lighthouse Media Centre in Wolverhampton.

NATIONAL CONVENTION OF PENSIONERS
20th October 1986

It was the first time in history that the Pensioners National Convention took place in Wolverhampton. It was held at the Civic Hall, and was followed by a large number of people taking part in a rally in the town centre. More than seven hundred delegates from all over the country took part at the convention at which the chief guest was Jack Jones, a very well known national personality. He was a life-long trade unionist who had dedicated his whole life to getting the best for working class people. He held many offices with the trades union movement and was TUC General Secretary from 1966-78. One time he was regarded as a more powerful man than the Prime Minister.

After his retirement in 1978, he became the Pensioners' Champion, demanding fair deal for pensioners with better retirement pensions, heating allowance, bus passes and a free TV licence. It was a great honour for me to receive such a great person and other distinguished guests to Wolverhampton and it was a matter of great pride for me to sit on the stage with him at the Civic Hall. After the convention was over I received him at the Parlour along with some other VIPs such as the Bishop of Wolverhampton, Christopher Mayfair, Sam Clarke (President of the local pensioner's convention), Councillor George Howell, the past mayor of the town and other dignitaries. I was delighted to devote a full day in his company at the pensioner's convention at the civic hall and at my Parlour. During the time I had an excellent opportunity to have talk openly with him about his fascinating life, the various trades union struggles and his work for pensioners rights.

Throughout the whole period I found him most sincere, open, honest and down-to-earth with a decidedly humorous side to his personality. His inspiring generosity and decency was beyond description and unquestionable.

Proudly posing with Jack Jones (far right) in the Mayor's parlour after the National Convention of Pensioners—one of the most memorable days of my time as Mayor of Wolverhampton.

COLD ALERT SAYS JACK

T&G RECORD

Stop the old from freezing

A STATE of emergency to prevent old people freezing to death in one of the coldest spells for over 25 years was demanded last month by Jack Jones, president of the T&G Retired Members' Association.

He condemned the government's payments system as "totally inadequate with rules that must have been written by a descendent of Scrooge."

Speaking on the ITV news he said: "The government should declare an emergency. They should say that all people in receipt of supplementary benefit will immediately get £5 a week during the cold weather, and that all oth ld people will get assistance.

"i ne situation is sufficiently important to justify the police being used to contact every old person to make sure they are warm, that they have good heating, good clothes and adequate food."

OUTRAGE

Earlier at a pensioners' rally and march in Liverpool he stressed: "Thousands of pensioners face death this winter unless something is done to keep them warm in their homes.

"It is an outrage that we pay more to heat shops and offices than homes of people who

Turning them out in Wolverhampton

WELL OVER 700 pensioners attended a rally in Wolverhampton which was addressed by Jack Jones, pictured with the mayor Bishan Dass and his wife, and Sam Clarke, RMA regional chairman for the midlands, who organised the rally and another in Walsall.

The mayor was a bus worker for several years and a member of Wolverhampton's 5/6 branch of the T&G.

HANDS ACROSS BRITAIN

In the mid 1980s the Borough of Wolverhampton was suffering unprecedented high unemployment of 21% compared with 17% nationally. Some of the wards with a high concentration of ethnic minorities population suffered a disproportionately higher percentage of unemployment where more than 33% were out of work, with some of them out of work for more than a year. In the circumstances of hopelessness and underlying racial inequality and prejudice, the prospect of full employment appeared to be minimal. The presumption was that the blacks are the last to find employment and the first to be dispensed with should circumstances dictate a reduction in staffing levels.

I have been an active trade unionist for the whole of my life and I have been actively involved in many campaigns organised by trade unions and community organisations against deprivation, racial prejudice and the ever-increasing unemployment situation. The March For Jobs in 1971 and the miners' strike of 1974 are two of the most memorable experiences of my life. I am proud to have taken an active part in both the marches and campaigned for worker's rights. I still have lots memories of those historical struggles and I still have some souvenirs such as a mug from 1971 march, depicting on it the Liverpool to London March For Jobs, and a book with detailed illustrations and pictures of the miners' strike of 1974. I am pleased to print some information opposite about the activities taking place at that time to highlight the plight of the unemployed.

HANDS
ACROSS
BRITAIN

Southbank House
Black Prince Road
London SE1 5S.

Tel: 01-582 8256

Revd. Michael Godfrey
283, Henwood Road
Wolverhampton
West Midlands
WV6 8FU
Wolverhampton 752278

MG/JS

19th May, 1987

Dear Mr. Mayor,

Thank you for taking part in the Hands Across Britain press conference on Wednesday 15th April. I hope you considered the press conference was worthwhile. I felt it did make some contribution to attracting publicity for the event on 3rd May. It also showed the commitment of yourself and your Council to the problem of unemployment and to the plight of the unemployed.

You will be interested to know that we estimated that probably 3,000 people took part in the Walsall section fo the Hands Across Britain. Although this was less than required I think this was a particular achievement recognising that our Committee only had two months to organise the event. It proved exceptionally difficult to attract media publicity. Only with massive media coverage before the event could Hands Across Britain have been a complete success. Thank you, therefore, for your contribution.

You may be interested to know that we are planning a public meeting on 26th June on the theme of "Unemployment - What should the new Government now do?" This, we hope, will take place in Walsall with a panel of speakers representing various sections of our local life. I would be grateful if you could pass on information about this to your colleagues.

Yours sincerely,

Revd. Preb. Michael Godfrey,
Chairman of the Wolverhampton/Walsall
Committee

Mr. Bishan Dass,
Mayor of Wolverhampton,
Civic Centre,
Wolverhampton.

MAYOR'S PARLOUR
2 1 MAY 1987
RECEIVED

WOLVERHAMPTON MARATHON
5th April 1987

The Wolverhampton Marathon has a long history going back to 1982 and it was an annual event until 1987. Thereafter it was discontinued (due to funding difficulties) until 1998 when it was resurrected. The 1987 event was organised by the Wolverhampton Marathon Management Committee headed by Billy Wilson who runs the popular Tettenhall Horse Sanctuary. As Mayor of the town I took a keen interest in some of the promotional activities for the event and I was asked at one point, a week before the race to pose for photos in a track suit with the insignia around my neck.

The press photographer and some other people were present in the Parlour when I agreed to pose for the photo and changed into my track suit. I asked Paul Allen, my attendant, to fetch the insignia and he went around to the office and asked the secretary but she would not let him bring the insignia and he returned empty handed. I sent him back and kept waiting for at least twenty minutes before eventually the secretary came over, looking very angry, with the medallion in her hands. She passed it to me, gave me a very rude look and returned to her office. I felt insulted publically in front of the others but I suppressed my feeling for the time being and carried on with what I was preparing to do. After I finished my engagement and everyone had gone I called my secretary into my working office and asked her to call the Chief Executive. She asked me *"What for?"* I said *"I want to have word a with him."* She said *"What about?"* *"Something personal"* I replied. She returned to her office without saying anything. After waiting for few more minutes, I called her again to my office and asked if Mr Lion, the Chief Executive, is coming. *"He is not available at the moment"*, she replied. *"OK, will you please try again after a few minutes"*, I said. Her facial expression depicted deep anger and an attitude of non-compliance. She stormed back to her office without saying anything. After waiting for few minutes, I phoned the Chief Executive's office and enquired of his PA whether Mr Lion is in the office and the reply was, *"Yes he is".* "Can I have quick word with him?", I said. I asked him to come to my office and he came around straight away. I called the secretary and told Mr Lion what had happened and told him that I am not going to tolerate this kind of behaviour any more. She was feeling shaken and said sorry and apologised to me and promised to listen to me in future. Mr. Lion advised her that she is there to look after the Mayor and performed her responsibilities according to her job description. In the end the photograph appeared in the newspaper and was much commented on.

I had the privilege of starting the 1987 marathon from the point at the ring road between Wolverhampton University (then Polytechnic) and the Molineux football ground. There were over 5,000 runners from all over the country and some from abroad also took part. Among the popular (at that time) participants was the now dishonoured Jimmy Saville who had been invited to performed the opening of the renal unit for kidney patients at the New Cross hospital. Following the conclusion of the race I organised a reception for the marathon committee and some VIPs in the Mayor's Parlour. On the following pages, I have printed some of the very interesting pictures of myself posing for press photos to promote the marathon and Billy Wilson putting me on my mark and the others press coverage showing the starting of the 1987 marathon on 5th April 1987.

WOLVERHAMPTON
MARATHON '87 SPECIAL

An Express & Star souvenir

EXPRESS AND STAR, MONDAY, APRIL 6, 1987

Everyone's a winner on carnival day out

NEARLY 5,000 runners pounded the streets of Wolverhampton for its sixth marathon spectacular — and every one of them was a winner.

Thousands of people lined the streets to cheer their grit and determination as they covered every painful yard of the 26-mile course.

For once the sun smiled on the event, with runners and spectators alike responding to the pleasant spring weather as the competitors struggled to the finishing line.

The heart of the town was transformed for just a day into a carnival atmosphere.

204

Hero Doug's victory

STORIES: David Knight, Bryan Summers, David Fenton PICTURES: Geoff Wright, David Bagnall

205

Billy Wilson's order was "On Your marks, Mr Mayor" in order to promote the 1987 Wolverhampton Marathon.

INTERNATIONAL AFFAIRS

Although I have concentrated on some of the local activities that I undertook as Mayor of Wolverhampton I did also play an important role in ensuring that the town's voice was heard right around the globe:

There was a number of international issues that people in the town were concerned about. I personally have always taken a keen interest in subjects involving international politics, equality, and human rights. There were burning issues in several countries such as India, Chile, Rhodesia (now Zambia), South Africa and many others at that time that people like myself were deeply concerned about. Below are just some of them:

SOWETO TENTH ANNIVERSARY

A joint meeting was held on 16th June 1986, at the Dunkley Street Learning and Resources Centre to mark the tenth anniversary of the Soweto Massacre in South Africa. A number of organisations from the town took part and after some impassioned speeches the following resolution was passed unanimously:

> On the occasion of the 10th Anniversary of the SOWETO MASSACRE, we remember those who died at Soweto and all who died since fighting for human rights in South Africa.
> We the undersigned call upon the South African government to end apartheid now and to avoid the inevitable bloodbath which will follow refusal to do so. And we call upon the British Government to implement immediate sanctions against South Africa in accordance with the United Nations resolution.

SPONSERED AND SIGNED BY :-
Councillor John Bird leader, signed on behalf the Labour councillors of Wolverhampton.
Councillor Bishan Dass the Mayor of Wolverhampton for the year 1986/87.
Mr. E. Warner (Wolverhampton community relations council)
Mr. Naranjan Singh Noor (Indian Workers Association)
Mr. George Barnsley (Freedom March organiser, Wolverhampton)
Trades council Wolverhampton
African National Congress, Wolverhampton branch.
Many community and religious organisations of the town

It was followed by a protest march in the town centre in which over 1000 people took part and leaflets were distributed.

CHILE

Ruled by the military dictator Pinochet, every day out of Chile were coming horrible stories of oppression, killings and shootings. The whole world was raising its voice against the atrocities that were taking place in Chile and asking for the reinstatement of democracy. In Wolverhampton George Barnsley used to go around the town centre every Saturday with a loud-speaker on his car shouting slogans against the military dictatorship in Chile and it was clear that other residents of Wolverhampton—like other people through the world— were equally concerned with the situation in Chile. In my capacity as the Mayor of the town, I wrote a letter to the Chilean embassy highlighting the concern of people here and asking for the reinstatement of democracy in order to bring an end to the atrocities. Below is a copy of the letter I wrote but unfortunately had no reply as the military dictators were not responding to any public opinion in the world.

MAYOR'S PARLOUR
CIVIC CENTRE
ST PETER'S SQUARE
WOLVERHAMPTON
WV1 1RG

TELEPHONE N° 27611

29 September 1986

Dear Sir

We are writing to you on behalf of the people of Wolverhampton in order to express our deep concern for the life of opposition leaders, priests and students imprisoned under the regulations of State of Siege enforced in your country after the assassination attempt on General Pinochet.

We strongly condemn the reprisals taken by government supporters against opponents of the regime, which have cost so far the life of journalist Jose Carrasco, Gaston Vidaurrazaga and Felipe Rivera.

Furthermore, we feel an obligation as British people towards the fate of Cesar Bunster, who lived and was educated in this country, and ask you to make sure that should he be found:

(a) he is not shot on sight;

(b) he is not tortured;

(c) he is given a fair trial at which international observers are present.

We look forward to the day when the democracy is restored to Chile.

Yours faithfully

Bass.

Mayor

Councillor J A W Bird,
Leader of the Council.

Chilean Ambassador
Chilean Embassy
12 Devonshire Street
LONDON W1.

SOUTH AFRICA

I wrote both to the South African Ambassador in London and Margaret Thatcher, our Prime Minister. The responses make interesting reading. The first document is from the South African Ambassador:

"Dear Councillor Dass,

I refer to your recent letter which was addressed to the Ambassador.

The South African Government is committed to a policy of genuine power sharing amongst all the peoples in the country and President P. W. Botha rejected 'apartheid' on 31 January 1986 when he stated that South Africa has "outgrown the outdated colonial system of paternalism as well as the outdated concept of apartheid". The specific policies to which president Botha is striving are:

- an undivided South Africa where all regions and communities within its boundaries form part of the South African state with the right to participate in institutions to be negotiated collectively:

- the sovereignty of the law as the basis for the protection of the fundamental rights of individuals and groups:

- that any future system must conform with the requirements of a civilised legal system and ensure access to the courts and equality before the law:

- the protection of human dignity, life, liberty and property of all regardless of colour, race, creed or religion:

- a negotiated democratic system of government accommodating all political aspirations of all South

African communities and:
- that all South Africans must be placed in a position where they can participate in government through their elected representatives.
To implement these policies President Botha has called on the leaders of the various Black communities to enter into a process of negotiation with the Government. He has, furthermore, made it clear that the agenda for these negotiations are open and that he would not prescribe who may attend.
I take this opportunity of listing a few of the areas where reform has already taken place or is due to take place as soon as it is practicable:

- Sport	:	*Open to all races*
- Labour union	:	*Modern, sophisticated trade system open to all races*
- Prohibition of Mixed Marriages Act	:	*Repealed*
- Immorality Act	:	*Offensive racial provision repealed*
- Immigration	:	*Provisions providing for white immigration repealed*
- Influx Control and Pass Laws	:	*Repealed on 1 July 1986*
- Constitutional	:	*Asians and Coloureds represented in Parliament*
	:	*Asians and Coloureds holding Ministerial and Deputy Ministerial positions in the Government*
	:	*Legislation providing for a*

211

		National Council tabled in Parliament as interim measure for Black participation in Government until a new Constitutional framework has been negotiated
	:	Universal franchise accepted
- Public Amenities	:	Continued existence of Separate Amenities Act under investigation by State President's Council
	:	All race restrictions in hotels, restaurants and accommodation establishments scrapped
- Forced resettlement	:	Discontinued
- Property rights for Blacks	:	Accepted as well as permancy of Black communities in urban areas
- Provisional Government	:	White elected Provisional Government scrapped on 1 July 1986. Replaced by an appointed multi-racial executive committee
- Local Government	:	Full participation of all communities

This list is not exhaustive or in any specific order. I include it in this letter simply to indicate that the South African Government has not been dilatory in carrying out

212

its reform programme.

Your call for sanctions and boycotts should also be compared to the result of a recent survey, conducted on behalf of the Ford Foundation by professor Fatima Meer of the Institute of Black Research in Durban. In the survey Professor Meer found that no more than 26 per cent of the respondents would support disinvestment if it meant that "many people lost their jobs".

It should be noted in this regard that Professor Meer was one of the most vocal critics of the similar findings of a 1984 survey, which had been conducted by professor Lawrence Schlemmer into the views of Black production workers, and that Professor Meer can certainly not be accused of having an anti-sanctions view.

I am sure that you are also aware that the legitimacy of a free and active trade union movement has long been recognised in South Africa. In fact, the system of labour relations in the country is widely regarded as one of the most modern in the world. Consequently, I can assure you that any trade unionist detained in terms of the security legislation is not being detained because of bona fide trade union activity. It is, however, regrettable that trade unions in South Africa do find themselves in the unfortunate position of having a political role because the pace of socio-economic reform has outpaced that of political reform.

Finally I would like to register my disappointment at the fact that your Council saw its way clear to approve a resolution of this nature without allowing this Embassy to state the South African case. Surely it would have been in the best interests of objectivity to have done so?

Yours sincerely

The second response came from the British Foreign & Commonwealth Office on behalf of the Prime Minister, Margaret Thatcher. The letter included a document setting out the British Government's position on South Africa:

Introduction

South Africa's internal problems have aroused great concern and interest among the world community. The Government's policy has long to be to work, together with our EC and Commonwealth partners, for fundamental change in South Africa. We want this change to be brought about peacefully without violence and by dialogue and reform, not revolution.

Our attitude to Apartheid

We wish apartheid to be brought to an end at the earliest possible date. We want to see established in its place a non-racial society with democratic, representative government and with proper safeguards for all minorities. Only that can be the secure foundation of a prosperous South Africa, living in harmony with its neighbours . We have impressed upon the South African Government the urgent need for fundamental reform to remove discrimination and to prepare the way for the establishment of a system of government which commands the support of the people of South Africa as a whole. With the aim of sending a clear political signal to the South African Government, Her Majesty's Government has for years followed a policy of both restrictive and positive measures.

Restrictive Measures

Restrictive measures have covered not only arms sales

and sporting contacts, where we were bound by international agreements, but also a general refusal to collaborate in the military and nuclear fields.

In September 1985 we consolidated the measures we were taking in a package agreed with our Community partners:

- we do not trade in arms with South Africa:
- we have no military co-operation and have withdrawn our Military Attachés from Pretoria;
- we do not export oil:
- we do not export sensitive equipment which could be used for repressive purposes by the Police or Armed Forces:
- we do not collaborate with South Africa in nuclear development:
- we have from the outset observed the 1977 Gleneagles Agreement discouraging sporting links.

Further restrictive measures were agreed by the Commonwealth Heads of Government at Nassau in October 1985:

- a ban on all new Government loans to the South African Government and its agencies:
- a readiness to take unilaterally what action may be possible to preclude the import of Krugerrands (the import of all gold coins from South Africa has now been banned by the British Government):
- an end to Government funding for trade missions to South Africa and for participation in exhibitions and trade fairs.

Additional measures agreed by the United Kingdom at

the Commonwealth Review Meeting in London in August
1986:
- a voluntary ban on new investment in South Africa:
- a voluntary ban on the promotion of tourism in South
Africa.

In September 1986 all European Community member
states agreed to ban new investment in South Africa and
the import of iron, steel and gold coins from South Africa.

<u>Positive Measures</u>
We have complemented these restrictive measures with
<u>positive</u> steps on the premise that the economic advance-
ment of Blacks is a prime motor for political change and
for the ultimate elimination of apartheid:
- in 1977 we took the lead in drawing up a European
Community Code of Conduct for companies with interests
in South Africa. The Code sets out guidelines for good
employer practices covering, for example, trade unions,
migrant labour, pay, fringe benefits, and desegregation.
With our European partners we have recently strengthened and improved the Code which remains voluntary. It
now covers additional matters including company
involvement in community projects and the promotion of
black businesses:
- British companies have created jobs for over 100,000
black workers in South Africa, providing support for an
estimated five times that number in the black
community. They also give direct assistance to
educational programmes, technical training and
community housing for blacks.
- our aid programme is directed mainly at providing

English language training and student scholarships for non-white South Africans (almost £1.6 million in 1985/86):
- the Prime Minister announced in July 1986 a new commitment of £15.75 million over 5 years, mainly for education and training:
- on 16 September 1986 EC Foreign Ministers undertook to strengthen and improve co-ordination of their programme of positive measures.

General Economic Sanctions
The Government is firmly opposed to general economic and trade boycotts because we believe they would hold back, not advance, the achievement of the objectives set out above. We understand why many have called for full economic sanctions against South Africa as a means to force the pace of change. But we believe that calls for general sanctions are misconceived, and fail to take into account the real consequences of such action. In the Government's view, the effect of such sanctions, which would have to be left in place for many years would be:
- to stiffen the South African Government's resistance to change; it would also be forced into a position of greater self-reliance:
- to worsen the cycle of frustration, violence and repression; (because sanctions would raise false expectations of early change and, as they took effect, would hit the black population hardest):
-to undermine further the stability of the region (because they would seriously weaken neighbouring African economies):
- to damage UK interests in South Africa and increase

unemployment in the UK.

South African Government's Reform Programme
We much regret that the South African Government has not moved more quickly towards the total abolition of apartheid. But it would be wrong to dismiss all the reforms which have been announced by the South African Government in recent months as irrelevant. We welcome for example:
- abolition of the Pass Laws:
- repeal of much petty apartheid:
- suspension of forced resettlement:
- ending of almost all job reservation on a racial basis:
- restoration of South African citizenship to Blacks resident outside the "independent" homelands:
- granting of freehold property rights to Blacks:
- introduction of uniform identity documents for all races:
- lifting of restrictions on black small businesses.

Such reforms are not to be discounted. But they do not go to the heart of the problem. The South African Government has yet to convince the world community that they are addressing the fundamental issues of black political rights in South Africa and the total abandonment of the concept of separate development.

RECENT DEVELOPMENTS
Commonwealth Group of Eminent Persons
The Commonwealth Eminent Persons Group was set up by the Commonwealth Governments at Nassau in October 1985.m The Group's objective was to seek ways of promoting dialogue with South Africa and a

218

suspension of violence. It was a great disappointment that the members of the Group were not able to achieve what they set out to do. But they nevertheless showed considerable resolve in their task. Future initiatives will build on the course charted by the Commonwealth Group.

Meetings with the ANC
The Government condemns violence whoever perpetrates it:
- we acknowledge that the ANC is an important focus for black opinion in South Africa:
- we have established Ministerial level contact with the ANC leadership in the course of which we impressed upon the ANC our view that a suspension of violence <u>on all sides</u> is essential to the creation of a climate in which dialogue and negotiation can become possible.

European Council 26-27 June
At their meeting in the Hague at the end of June the European Council of Ministers voiced their concern at the restrictions imposed under the State of Emergency and the indiscriminate arrest of thousands of South Africans (the Government had earlier made strong bilateral representations to there South African Government in London and Pretoria).
The European Governments again called for the unconditional release of all political prisoners including Nelson Mandela, and for the lifting of the ban on the African National Congress, the Pan Africanist Congress of Azania and other political parties.
In the meantime it was agreed that in the three months

following the European Council's meeting the Community would enter into consultations with other industrialised countries on further measures which might need covering, in particular a ban on new investments, the import of coal, iron, steel and gold coins from South Africa.

The European Council asked the British Foreign Secretary to visit Southern Africa in his capacity as President of the Council in a further effort to establish conditions in which the necessary dialogue could begin. He did so at the end of July. It is much to be regretted that the response of the South African Government was not such as to contribute to the progress of the kind which we and other European Governments sought.

Commonwealth Review meeting 3-5 August

Against this background the Commonwealth Heads of Government Review Meeting was held in London. It reaffirmed the united belief that "apartheid must be dismantled now if a greater tragedy is to be averted, and that concerted pressure must be brought to bear to achieve that end."

Although unanimity on the question of measures against South Africa was not possible, the United Kingdom joined the other six Commonwealth Governments in issuing a joint statement of principles and agreed to take certain further measures (listed above) to demonstrate continuing concern at the situation in South Africa and our wish to work with our Commonwealth and European partners for an urgent and peaceful political solution.

European Foreign Affairs Council 15-16 September

At their meeting in Brussels in September, the Foreign

Ministers of the Twelve once again called strongly on the South African Government to facilitate a national dialogue and in particular to release unconditionally Nelson Mandela and other political prisoners and to lift the ban on the ANC, PAC and other political parties. They reiterated the importance of positive measures to assist the victims of apartheid. They also adopted a new package of restrictive measures consisting of bans on new investment and the import of iron, steel and gold coins from South Africa. The Presidency undertook to continue to seek consensus among the twelve on the question of a ban on the import of coal from South Africa.

OVERSEA VISITORS

During my year as Mayor I was delighted to receive a variety of overseas visitors to the Mayor's Parlour. One of the most agreeable groups were a party of students from Moscow who were undertaking a course at Wolverhampton Polytechnic's School of Languages. After their visit I received the letter and photograph overleaf.

ZEEBRUGGE FERRY TRAGEDY
3rd March 1987

The Zeebrugge Ferry tragedy of 1987 touched the heart of every one in this country and at the full council meeting on Wednesday 11th March 1987, members were asked to rise and observe a minute's silence for all those had perished in this terrible accident. On behalf of people of Wolverhampton I also extended our

221

Le Bourg,
Campagnac-les-Quercy,
F-24550 Villefranche-du-Périgord.
May 12ᵗʰ, 1987

Dear Mr Mayor,

I should like to thank you once again for the reception you gave to the young visitors from Moscow. The visit was extremely successful as was our visit to Moscow and Yaroslavl', where we were all invited to private homes. Everywhere we had very interesting and frank discussions. In fact Yaroslavl' might be a very suitable partner, if the town makes application for a town twinning Lambeth seems to have gone ahead with its partnership with the Moskovoretsky district of Moscow. There was even a programme devoted to it on Central (Moscow) Television while we were there.

deepest sympathy and condolences to the passengers and crew of the ferry " Herald of Free Enterprise" and their families.

I made a public appeal for Ferry Disaster Fund and it had a very positive spontaneous response from the public here. Donations both large and small came from individuals and organisations alike—the photo shows the contribution of the Federation of Youth Service Music Groups who raised £495.14 for the fund.

INVITATION FROM INDIA

I have mentioned earlier that I attended more that 2,300 engagements during my year of mayoralty and I had the opportunity to meet and receive at the Parlour, many prominent personalities, political, religious, community and trade union leaders during my year in office. Sometimes they would respond by inviting me to visit them. Amongst these invitations was one to visit India as the guest of honour of the Mayor of New Delhi. Unfortunately I had to decline all such invitations due to my busy schedule and I was very sensitive about not providing any opportunity for anyone to criticise me for spending taxpayers money on such visits.

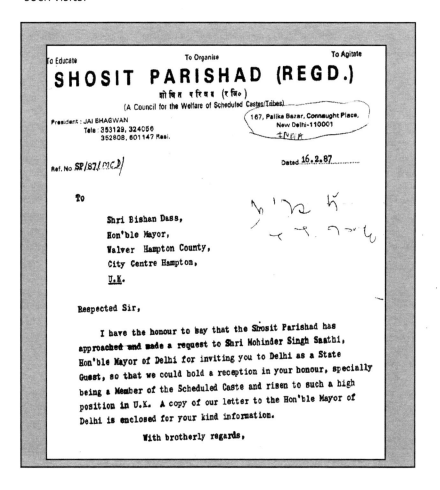

THE SAGA OF CLINTON McCURBIN

During my year of mayoralty, an unfortunate incident took place which damaged race relations and community cohesion in the town. On 20th. Feb. 1987 a young West Indian man named Clinton McCurbin died while being arrested for allegedly using a stolen credit card in one of the shops in Dudley Street, Wolverhampton. He died of asphyxia while being restrained by the police in the shop.

The black and ethnic minority communities were outraged at the excessive force used by the police. Relations between the police and black ethnic minorities were not very congenial at the time, due to some degree by a lack of trust, which had already damaged their relationship. After this incident their attitude towards the police further hardened and many black youngsters roamed the town centre looking for an opportunity for revenge against the police. This incident sparked some disturbances and created racial tension in the town with the whole situation became extremely volatile as the police were blamed for being anti-black and of using unreasonable force.

A number of organisations in the town gathered together and organised a protest march. More than 1,500 people marched through the town centre on a very cold day of high wind and snow. The incident gave rise to even greater tension and tempers were close to spilling over. There was a sigh of relief when the march passed off peacefully with only a few skirmishes with the police. I was deeply concerned about the racial tension in the town and I was extremely mindful of my position as Mayor whilst belonging to an ethnic minority community. It was obviously not

225

appropriate for me as the Mayor to take sides or be anywhere near the demonstration.

However, as Mayor, I was interested to know what was taking place in the town. I put on my wellington boots, scruffy jeans and hoody coat (totally covering my head and face) and being fully camouflaged I set off for the town centre. Instead of going in the official chauffer drive car, I travelled by bus and soon I was standing at a bus stand in Cleveland Street waiting for the march coming from the side of School Street. The march entered Cleveland Street surrounded by a massive police presence. I started walking along the demonstrators to have a first-hand view and to witness the whole situation. After walking a few yards, I saw Nick Budgen MP walking along as well, *"Hallo Mr. Budgen"*, I said. He expressed great surprise to see me there. By now the march turned into Market Street by the Central Library, and there was a short hold up by the Queen Street traffic lights. I was standing next to the Primark Store and I spoke to one of the senior police officers, enquiring politely, *"What is happening at the front officer?"* There was no reply, he avoided answering and instead I was pushed and shoved to the side, *"Come on move....move on"* he shouted. A hotdog seller close by recognised me, *"He is the Mayor"*, she shouted. The police officer turned around, looked at me, and reluctantly apologised to me, saying *"Sorry sir"* before walking away. .

In my capacity as Mayor of the town, I appealed for harmony and unity amongst the residents of Wolverhampton. In my open letter, I said the recent tragic death of a young man has opened up old wounds and revived suspicions and recriminations and a few opportunists have exploited all that. Since I took over the office of mayoralty the previous May I had been encouraged

Mayor issues appeal for unity

The Mayor of Wolverhampton today issued a plea to townspeople to "pull together" as a united community in the aftermath of Clinton McCurbin's death.

Councillor Bishan Dass said in an open letter: "The recent tragic death has opened up old wounds and revived suspicions and recriminations, all fuelled and exploited by a few opportunists."

He said that since he became Mayor last May, he had been encouraged by the multi-cultural harmony being fostered by townspeople.

"That harmony has been built on the steady, unselfish commitment by the various communities and groups that make up the fabric of Wolverhampton.

"Their efforts have not only led to a town where people could live and work happily together, they were beginning to reassure the business community outside the boundaries that Wolverhampton was a steadily prospering force.

Succeed

"All this work to create a healthy image for the town must not be squandered now.

"We must harness the goodwill built up in the past. We must all pull together and face the future united and unswerving in our determination to succeed," he added.

Meanwhile, the police chief leading the probe into Mr McCurbin's death issued a new appeal today for witnesses.

Det Chief Supt David Cole said that his inquiry team had already interviewed 115 people.

But he is anxious to contact several other onlookers who may be able to supply vital evidence to the Police Complaints Authority probe.

In particular, he wants to speak to an elderly couple who "had a good look" at the incident in the Next clothes shop, where Mr McCurbin died in a struggle with two policemen.

"We have information from other witnesses who described seeing an elderly couple outside the shop," said Mr Cole.

Shopping

"They remained there for some time having a good look through the door of the shop and we believe they witnessed the actual incident."

He described the couple as in their late 60s, about 5ft 2in, wearing overcoats and hats, and carrying shopping bags.

Mr Cole urged the couple to contact police and stressed that their identities would be kept secret and their information treated in confidence.

He said he was also trying to trace three people quoted in newspaper reports as having seen the incident.

They are: Mrs Marion Wheeler, quoted in the Sunday Express; Mr Paul Brown, who gave an interview to Today; and Mr Jimmy Foster, who spoke to the Express and Star. None gave addresses.

Mr Cole repeated an appeal to three other witnesses — a girl customer in her 30s, an elderly black woman and a "mild-mannered" black man.

by the multi-culturalism and racial harmony being fostered by the townspeople. We had many different communities and groups who were making a steady and unselfish commitment to achieve just harmony amongst us all.

Their efforts had not only led to a town where people can live and work happily together in harmony, they were beginning to reassure the business community outside the town boundaries that Wolverhampton was a steadily prospering force. And not all the work to create such a healthy image for the town could be squandered now. We had to harness the goodwill built in the past. We had to all pull together and face the future united with a firm determination to succeed.

The Labour Party which controlled the council constantly reviewed law and order, and the community cohesion situation in the town. The Labour group considered a proposition to provide a £10,000 grant to an organisation that was fighting the legal case on behalf of McCurbin's family and who were seeking judicial review into the circumstances leading to the tragic incident.

There were differences of opinion and the Labour group was divided on this issue. The group discussed it and voted on it three times at their meeting. I was of the opinion that it was a most sensitive issue and any financial support by the council could be counter-productive and further damage race relations in the town. For this reason, I chose to abstain. Some of the group members were not happy with me as they expected me to support this motion. The proposal was put on the full council agenda and a heated discussion took place in the Council chamber. Members of the Council had an opportunity to have an full and open discussion regarding the incident and the situation concerning community cohesion and race relations in the town. It was a very sensitive issue in the very delicate circumstances. Any suggestion that financial help to pay for legal costs should be offered generated a great deal of controversy and public opposition. I was not whole-heartedly convinced and voted against the resolution.

The Council itself was bitterly divided on the resolution of granting of £10,000 to fight the legal case but eventually it was passed. This decision by the Labour-controlled council backfired during the next local elections and the Labour Party lost control of the Council. There were many shockwaves as some of the leading councillors—including myself— lost their seats at the next election.

After an inquest at the Crown Court which lasted seven days the jury returned a verdict of "Misadventure" and said that the police involved should face no criminal proceedings. This not only created a dent in race relations locally but also hardened the attitude of many black youngsters towards the police.

1987 LOCAL ELECTION

The 1987 elections took place on 4th May, and as usual the counting of votes took place at the Civic Hall on the same night. It was usual practice to announce results one by one at the Wulfrun Hall after the count in the Civic Hall. All the candidates had the opportunity to speak and say a few words after the announcement of the results. The counting of the votes for the Heath Town ward was completed at about midnight and the Returning Officer came onto the stage in the Wulfrun Hall to make the announcement. I was standing on the stage along with other candidates.

The Returning Officer announced the results and it became clear that I had lost to a Liberal party candidate. I had the opportunity to say few words but as soon as I moved close to the microphone, a mob of unruly youngsters in the Tory crowd started shouting insulting and racial abuse at me. They carried on using dirty and abusive words and were heckling and shouting in front of the stage, making an incredibly loud noise and demonstrating their uncivilised behaviour. They were determined not to let me speak but I was standing calmly on the stage with a gentle smile on my face. One of my Labour colleagues, Councillor Ray Garner, lost his temper and hurled something at the face of one of them who immediately fell on the floor. Councillor Garner was a short and heavy built person and it seemed very strange for him to act in this manner. There were some altercation and the police jumped in and separated them before drawing a dividing line between the Labour and the Tory members in order to keep both sides apart.

I was still standing cool on the stage and watching the whole melodrama taking place in front of my eyes. Then eventually everybody went quiet and there was a silence through-

230

out the hall. Now it was my turn to say something and everyone was looking curiously at me. I said, *"Ray you have not done the right thing, and I do not condone your actions. These are sick people; they do not need thumping, they need some medical treatment instead."*

I finished my short speech, moved to one side and slowly walked down the steps to join the Labour supporters standing in front of the stage. I was mobbed by a crowd of supporters, one by one hugging and shaking hands with me. They expressed commiserations and a great deal of sympathy for me, and deeply regretted that I had lost my seat. They still found it difficult to believe and digest that I had lost. Some of them with grim faces and tears in their eyes were hugging me repeatedly saying not much although their facial expressions were telling their own stories. I was deeply moved to see their affection and emotional sentiments for me.

Everybody was of the opinion that I have lost my seat due to Clinton McCurbin issue but In addition to the McCurbin saga, caste and religious prejudice played a significant role during the local elections, particularly in the Heath Town ward. The complexity of the Indian caste system and its effect on the political and social life of persons of Indian origin is beyond imagination. It is extremely difficult for people of the indigenous community to understand the gravity of the Indian caste system. India, since 1947, is now an independent democratic country. However, after six decades of elections in India, people still give priority to candidates belonging to their own caste and the majority of them vote the same way. Some of the Asians living abroad, particularly the elderly, follow the same pattern of voting as is generally practiced in India. Once again, politics of caste and religion played a significant role during local elections of 1987. There are a high percentage of Asian voters living in Heath Town who belong to different castes and religions. I know some of them found it difficult to swallow the pill and vote for a person not belonging to their caste. They preferred instead to vote for a Liberal candidate.

My defeat generated a mixed reaction amongst residents of Wolverhampton. Some regretted the loss of a dedicated and hard working councillor; some of them voiced concern about losing the lonely voice in the council chamber.

However, some celebrated my defeat by organising all-night parties in pubs and clubs. They had no hesitation in showing their emotions and the true colour of caste hatred and racial prejudice. As usual, they did not have the slightest shame about what they are actually doing. Instead, they rejoiced and celebrated glorifying the victory of egoism and caste prejudice.

I had no regret in losing the seat but I was aggrieved and deeply hurt by the way and the underlying reasons that I had lost the election. Thereafter I decided that I would never seek to contest a seat in order to be elected again to the Council. I did try my best to serve the people of my ward and the community of Wolverhampton at large according to the best of my ability and I found it difficult to compromise with some people for their philosophy of inequality and prejudice based upon caste and religion.

The unexpected results of the local elections appeared as headlines in every local newspaper. I received several letters of support following the shouting incident at the Wulfrun Hall and I have great pleasure in printing just some of the letters of support and press articles portraying the picture of 1987 elections:

Express & Star
Largest evening sale in the Midlands

Telephone (0902) 31 31 31   Friday, May 8, 1987

Wolverhampton drama: Tory John Mellor ousts Labour's Mrs Mel Chevannes; deputy leader Peter Bilson is defiant after polling leaves mayor Bishan Dass with the casting vote

LABOUR NOW CLINGING ON

The newspapers were full of the story of how Labour had suffered significant losses in the election of 1987. Seven senior Labour councillors—including myself—lost our seats, giving the Conservatives the opportunity to seize control of the Council.

Ad-News - 14-05-87

Mayor's vote is the key

Labour's defeated candidates

LABOUR MAULED

Bill Clarke: We attach great importance to vote on May 20.

Larry McClean: Waiting for the best offer.

Peter Bilson: Ousted from Labour leadership.

Labour were down, but not quite out, after last week's election onslaught by the Conservatives and the Alliance.

Seven Labour councillors lost their seats, leaving the council hung at 30-30.

But Labour believe they can hold on to power through the casting vote of Mayor Bishan Dass, although he has lost his seat.

His vote should allow Labour to choose the new mayor on May 20, thus maintaining their narrow advantage.

There was originally some confusion over the mayor's right to vote after losing his seat.

But Conservative leader Bill Clarke told the AdNews: "We will not protest the legality of the Mayor's casting vote, after having a full explanation of the situation by a council legal officer.

He said the Conservatives would nominate Coun. Mrs Doreen Seiboth for Mayor, with the support of the Alliance. Labour will nominate Coun. Phil Richards.

Coun. Clarke said: "We welcome the support of our Alliance members for our nomination and I would hope it is a sign

Seven go in election massacre

that their co-operation would make it possible to overcome Labour's control of this council.

"We attach great importance to the vote on May 20."

But Liberal leader Larry McClean was making no promises apart from their support for Coun. Sieboth.

He said: "Future support of the Alliance depends on which side takes control and we will wait to be approached by a party.

"We were elected as a separate group and will wait to make a decision until after May 20."

He would not comment on which side they would prefer to support - they would just wait for the best offer.

Another indirect victim of the election setback was Labour's acting leader, Peter Bilson.

In a secret ballot on Friday the Labour group passed him over and chose Coun Norman Davies as the new leader.

It is believed that Coun Bilson's controversial decision to pay the family's legal costs in the McCurbin case caused divisions in the Labour group. This allied to the election result may have cost Bilson the leadership.

Coun Davies was unavailable for comment at the time of going to press, but it is understood that he is confident Labour can elect the new mayor and continue in power.

This will mean great demands on former leader John Bird, who will have to be present for vital votes as well as continuing his duties as Euro MP.

Labour's defeated councillors were Neil Dougherty (Bilston North), Arthur Steventon (East Park), Mrs Mel Chevannes Reeves (Graiseley), Bishan Dass (Heath Town) Alan Garner (Spring Vale), Jim Woodward (Wednesfield North) and Ray Harding (Wednes-

Labour's defeated candidates

• Ray Harding

• Jim Woodward

• Mel Chevannes Reeves

• Neil Dougherty

• Arthur Steventon

• Bishan Dass

234

We Say

Dignity in the face of defeat

One incident from last week's election left a particularly nasty taste in the mouth.

That was the racist taunting of the Mayor, Bishan Dass, who had just lost his Heath Town seat.

In recent months this paper has not always been able to write complimentary stories about Labour candidates in Heath Town.

But in the case of Coun. Dass we would like to say a few words just for the record.

He has been an outstandingly good mayor, winning the respect and affection of all those he dealt with.

Racist harrassment reared its ugly head a few times during his year of office but he always behaved with good humour and dignity.

In short, he and his wife were superb ambassadors for our town.

For now, he is one of the victims of the dramatic anti-Labour swing in Wolverhampton but let us hope that he will be back one day.

Regardless of party politics, we need men of character on the council.

As for the morons who taunted him? They aren't really worth writing about.

Right-wing yobbos rubbish

We hear a lot about Left-wing Labour rowdies and loonies, but the Right-wing Tory supporters in the Civic Hall on the night of the Wolverhampton election results were a disgrace to any self-respecting community.

I have never seen such behaviour at an election count before. Is this going to be the pattern for the General Election? If so, I hope Labour supporters will behave with calm dignity like the Mayor, Bishan Dass, and treat these yobbos with the contempt they deserve. He was a gentleman, and they were rubbish.

One last point. The national and local Press are so jubilant regarding the Conservatives' showing over the local council elections that you would think the General Election was won for the Conservatives and was all over bar the shouting. Not so, Labour is still in there with a good chance of winning.

Harry Gomery,
Long Lake Avenue,
Tettenhall Wood,
Wolverhampton.

Now attack the vicious Right!

Perhaps the Express and Star would like to follow up its continuing campaign against the "Loony Left" with a few home truths about the loony — and vicious Right.

In the midst of your paper's undisguised glee at Labour discomfiture in the local elections, it was nevertheless revealed that "rowdies" with blue rosettes and Conservative stickers disrupted the announcement of results.

I attended the Wulfrun Hall that night and let no-one doubt that these Conservative supporters were extremists. The Conservative Party may claim to disown them now, but such elements operate freely on the Conservative Party's Right-wing and played their part in Conservative success.

At national and local level they wield increasing influence, as more moderate Conservatives must be well aware. That they are not speaking out is to their shame.

The Party claiming to stand for law and order and patriotism does itself no credit in tolerating, using and even encouraging such elements.

Likewise the Express and Star does itself no credit in exploiting every slip and smear it can use against the Labour Party, while consistently playing down the very real threat to democracy from extremists within and on the fringes of the Conservative Party.

Chris Irvine,
Mill Lane,
Wednesfield,
Wolverhampton.

A fine mayor

Sir,
May I add my appreciation of the Mayor, Mr Dass's work.

He and his family carried out their duties in a difficult year.

He is a most compassionate man, and I trust the new elected councillors will carry on his example for the good of the town, regardless of race and creed.

The good Lord made us all to be treated like human beings.

Thank you for your AdNews - the paper with the freedom to print.

Mrs M Seed
Kenilworth Crescent
Parkfields
Wolverhampton

Rare tribute

Sir,
May I congratulate you and indeed Mr Dass on your article in AdNews May 14, entitled "We Say Dignity in the face of defeat."

Such tribute to those who have served the Community well is all too rare in the Press.

Patience F Marshall
Rennaway Square,
Wolverhampton.

Just a few of the many letters published in the local papers in the aftermath of the election

1987 COUNCIL AGM

An unforgettable historical drama took place at the 1987 Annual General Meeting of the Council. After the local elections in May, both the Labour and Tory parties had 30 seats each, resulting in neither of the two main parties being able to claim a majority. In this situation, according to the constitution, the control of the council is dependent on the new Mayor's casting vote . Councillor Philip Richards the Mayor Elect of the Labour party were ready to take over the office of the Mayoralty. The Labour group had sorted out everything in order to take control of the council. At the Labour group meeting prior to the Council meeting, the leader of the Labour Party—Councillor John Bird— broke the sad news that one of our members was in hospital and was not going to be able to attend the meeting. Therefore, we were in the minority and consequently were not in a position to elect our Mayor and take control of the council. He advised everyone to keep this news strictly confidential until the very last minute. I had a full briefing about the circumstances and conduct of the meeting.

The Annual General Meeting of the Council started at 6.30pm at the Wulfrun Hall. The Tory Party entered having no knowledge of the emerging new situation where the Labour Party was in the minority. They were not aware that they were going to have a mayor of their party and they would be in control of the Council through the casting vote of the Mayor. I took the chair and started the proceedings of the meeting. I asked for nominations for mayor for the ensuing year. As usual, both the Labour and Tory parties put forward their nominations. The Labour party proposed Councillor Philip Richard and the Tory party proposed Councillor

Doreen Seiboth. The voting was taken by a show of hands which was counted by council officers. The results of count were handed over to me showing that the Labour Party candidate lost by 30 votes to 29. I announced the results, declaring councillor Doreen Sieboth the Mayor for the ensuing year. As soon as I made the announcement, there was confusion and utter pandemonium all throughout the hall. The members of the Tory party appeared to be baffled and they thought that I had made a mistake in announcing the results. They still did not know what had happened. There were whispering going all over the hall. I then invited councillor Doreen Seiboth to the dais to take the oath, go through the ceremonial mayor making, and then take control of the running of the rest of the meeting. She was very nervous and shaky because everything had happened so quickly. I provided her with some help to overcome this somewhat traumatic experience and supported her to conduct the rest of council meeting.

In my retiring mayor's speech, I highlighted a number of issues and problems that I had experienced during the year of my mayoralty:

> *"First of all, I would like to thank the mover and seconder of the vote of thanks for their kind comments. They are most welcome and my wife and I gladly receive them.*
> *Now I would like to turn to the municipal year of 1986/87, a year in which I had the great honour of serving the Borough of Wolverhampton as its Mayor and First Citizen.*
> *I must admit that my mayoralty hardly got off to the smoothest of starts. Controversy and argument unfortunately marred my inception as Mayor. It still grieves me that certain opportunists*

grieves me that certain opportunists were unable to resist an attempt to exploit and attack my nomination and to misinform and mislead the people of Wolverhampton. This I feel set the tone for a year which has seen the office of Mayor of Wolverhampton undermined and devalued on several occasions by people with little or no respect for the dignity of the mayoralty. This is something to which I will return later in my speech.

The theme which I adopted as Mayor, in keeping with 1986 as International Year of Peace, was "Equality, Liberty, Justice and Peace". This has constantly been to the forefront in my actions and speeches as Mayor. I was particularly pleased that the Council accepted the idea and naming of the peace Green off Waterloo Road. All these ideas remain very close to my heart. Without peace there is no life. Without equality, liberty and justice there can be no peace.

The most enjoyable duty throughout my year has been promoting the good name and reputation of Wolverhampton. I have endeavoured to do this to the best of my abilities at local, national and international levels. I have attended and addressed religious, social, political and community functions throughout the length and breadth of the United Kingdom, from Scotland to London. Indeed, a third of my time this year has been spent outside the boundaries of the Borough.

I have also taken very great pleasure in welcoming visitors from all over Great Britain and from countries such as Australia, Sweden, Kenya, the USSR, Canada, Uganda and Norway to name but a few.

In all of these encounters I have continually pointed to

the achievements of Wolverhampton and to all its positive attributes. I can't stress enough the great pleasure that this particular Mayoral duty has given me.

I also feel that my Mayoralty has done much to encourage the ethnic minorities in Wolverhampton to participate more actively and confidently in the life of the town. In particular , last year's Caribbean Focus I think was a great success. Also, encouraged by the role of the Mayoress, many more Asian women have become more confident and active within Wolverhampton.

I would like to make further comment on an area I raised at the beginning of my speech, in particular with reference to the running of Council meetings and the actions of elected members in the Council Chamber. There have been occasions when some people have shown total contempt for the people of Wolverhampton. In particular, the Standing Orders of the Council have suffered. I urge members strongly that if they truly believe in the mayoralty, they must do everything to protect the dignity of the Mayor, and the sanctity of the Standing Orders.

I have lived in Wolverhampton for 24 years, for 12 of those years I have been a Councillor I take great pride in the fact that I have been Mayor of this great Borough.

During the year I have often been asked by people where do I come from, what is my origin? My answer has always remained constant. I am from Wolverhampton and I am very proud to be a Wulfrunian. I have given the best years of my life so far in Wolverhampton and I intend to continue in the same vein, even if I am no longer a Councillor.

As I mentioned at the beginning, the start of my mayoralty had its unpleasant moments. So it is with regret that I have to say that the end too has had its share of unsavoury incidents. My defeat as a councillor has left me with a bitter taste in my mouth. I am not complaining about the fact that I lost an election, far from it; I am a

239

steadfast believer in democracy and the right of the people to decide. But I do feel bitter and saddened about the manner of the defeat.

As soon as I became Mayor I was bombarded with racist phone calls and letters. And so it has been that intolerance and prejudice have reared their ugly heads again during the local elections. The racism I experienced during and immediately after my own campaign was horrible.

Throughout my mayoralty such intolerance has at times made me think about my position within Wulfrunian society. And at times I must freely admit that I have been depressed. But I refuse to be discouraged by the views of a handful of racist extremists. I have also been able to draw solace and comfort from the very many letters and communications I have had in the course of the year congratulating me for my work on behalf of all the people of Wolverhampton. Indeed, only yesterday my wife and I received a letter from someone in Penn thanking us for the dignity which we have brought to the office of Mayor, and the valuable service which we have rendered to Wolverhampton.

But I feel that I must urge the wise men and women of this town to look very seriously at the issues of prejudice and intolerance. We must all work together to get rid of the evils of racism and inner city deprivation in order to achieve a harmonious and peaceful society.

I feel that I have said almost enough now. All that remains is for me to wholeheartedly acknowledge the invaluable assistance of my family, particularly my wife and daughter who have given me enormous support and accompanied me to most of my meetings. I'm grateful to the Officers of the Council who have assisted me greatly. I would also like to sincerely thank the staff of the Mayor's office who have done a most efficient and marvellous job. In particular the chauffeurs have always ensured that I have got to my functions on time, and have been excellent company on our long journeys together. I would also like to acknowledge the support of John Bird throughout my mayoralty. His advice and assistance was greatly appreciated and I hope that his expertise and experience will still be felt within Wolverhampton. Without all those people none of my achievements as Mayor of Wolverhampton over the past year would have been possible.

Finally, I would like to thank the people of Wolverhampton for receiving me so warmly wherever I went and for bestowing on me the greatest honour a citizen of this town can receive. All that remains now is for me to wish my successor well, and hope that she enjoys the challenges of mayoralty as greatly as I have done."

THE PERIOD FROM 1987 TO 2004

I remained out of the Council for 17 years after losing my seat for Heath Town ward. in 1987 Thereafter, I did not intend to return to the council as I felt I had enough of the it. I lost my seat, albeit unexpectedly, and for whatever reasons, which was a good enough excuse for me to say farewell to the Council for good. I regret to say here, that I was disappointed and deeply aggrieved by the behaviour and underlying   racial prejudice within the Labour Group. The agenda of equality within the Labour Party remained a theory on paper as against actual practice. I found it difficult to compromise and accept second-class treatment from my own party colleagues. I was not too happy about the way I was treated by the Labour Group members and its leaders.

I was not considered for any leading role such as chair of a Council committee and remained a backbencher for a long period of nine years. I raised this issue with the leader a few a times but felt I was a lonely voice lost amongst the crowd rubbing each other's backs. This issue of under- lying racial prejudice surfaced in 1983/84, when the Labour group continuously voted me out in the contest for mayoralty, thus breaking the established custom and practice over the past several years. And when I objected to this prejudicial treatment, I had threats of being thrown out of the party by removing the party whip. This proves that when you are a member of an organisation there is always the sword of discipline hanging over your head, waiting for an opportunity to exercise the right of execution. In these circumstances, you have very little choice between persecution and self-exile, and I preferred the second option. I thought it would be easy for me to expose the situation and take a more effective stand against racist elements from outside rather than being inside the Council.

However, you know, when you are addicted to something in your heart and soul it is extremely difficult to depart and live a life of isolation. I remained active at the grassroots level as member of the Labour Party and I served on a number of voluntary and community organisations. During this period, I devoted a great deal of my time with the All Saints Haque Centre (a welfare advice centre), the Bilston & Bradley Development Partnership, the Bilston Black Minority Ethnic Group and the Black Country Member's Numeration Committee to name but a few.

I was approached a few times by Labour Party members who asked me to return to the Council. There were people in the local community as well—particularly from the ethnic minorities—who would have liked to see me back in the Council chamber. However, I was not too keen to put myself into the same situation I had come out of few years ago, and endure humiliation and second-class treatment on ground of caste, colour and religion.

2004 LOCAL ELECTIONS

There were boundary changes in 2004 and an all-out election just as it had happened thirty years ago in 1973 when I was a candidate for the first time in Blakenhall ward. The Labour Party was looking for a number of people for the panel of candidates and some of the Party members approached me once again and asked to stand for the Council. In addition, at the time there was a great deal of pressure on me from the local community, in particular from members of the ethnic minorities, who would like to see me back in on the Council. I was unemployed at that time and very close to retiring age, and so I had some spare time to devote to such activities. In the circum-stances, I agreed to stand for the Wolverhampton City Council elections in May 2004. I was one of three candidates, the other two being Councillor Andrew Johnson and Councillor Alan Smith who were selected to contest the Ettingshall ward. It is a traditionally safe Labour seat, which we won without any problem. The result of voting was a bit of surprise, however, as I polled slightly more votes than my colleagues who had been on the Council for several years. This meant that I had the benefit of a four year term. I have served since then on several committees and scrutiny panels of the City Council and I was a member of the Licensing Committee and served as chair for several years (apart from a short break of few months when we briefly lost control of the council in 2008).

I thoroughly enjoyed my new council work compared with that in previous years. The management system of the council was slightly different as it had changed from committee style to cabinet responsibility and there was now stringent scrutiny involvement. The Council now had a fresh breed of members who had liberal approach and slightly more modern thinking compared with the old style proletariat socialists. It was a very different environment from not only the administration point of view but also the perception and thinking of elected members and the attitude of employees appeared to have transformed for better. Sadly, though, although there appeared to be a great deal of pressure from the national Labour Party to achieve a fair gender balance the aspirations and perceptions of colleagues from ethnic minorities are still often over looked.

Wolverhampton now had a 36% ethnic population and 15 out of 60 elected members of the council are from minority groups. Although the quality of ethnic members in some way is disappointing one or two of them like Councillor, Elias Mattu (now a cabinet member) are working closely with the community and responding positively to their interests.

Councillor Elias Mattu

I would like to mention here that in the old days people used to be interested enough to put themselves forward as a councillor with the single motive of providing voluntary services to the community. They used to have the ideology, commitment and dedication to bring about changes to improve the living conditions for the better. They were not concerned about personal gain apart, perhaps, from the status of being an elected member of the Council. The Council members were paid a meagre £13 attendance allowance per Council meeting. There was no special responsibility allowance or other benefits. This may be the reasons people were less concerned about achieving such positions as the chair or vice chair of any of the standing committees of the Council. The newly elected members had to undergo induction and training to learn the basics of the administration and managing and running the Council. In addition, they were required to learn about how to represent their constituents and to deal with individual casework. However, regrettably certain members often ran before they could walk and started looking for portfolios with better financial gains attached to the positions.

The old concept of serving the community has been taken over to some extent by personal gain. Previously people were less concerned about positions and financial incentives. Now there appears to be a tug of war for positions and portfolios such as cabinet and committee chairs of the council. This has not only created different tiers of councillors but has also generated a certain degree of deviation and egoism amongst elected members.

In addition to serving on the council, I was involved with a number of voluntary and community organisations. Some of these

your**LABOUR**
candidates

vote
Labour

ETTINGSHALL | Bishan Dass [X] | Andrew Johnson [X] | Alan Smith [X]

Polls open 7am - 10pm, Wolverhampton City Council Elections Thursday 10th June 2004

Your Labour Team of councillors, Andrew Johnson and Alan Smith will be joined in this election by the local community campaigner Bishan Dass. Bishan will strengthen the Labour Team and will enable your councillors to extend their efforts for the benefits of our new areas of Sedgemoor Park and All Saints. All three are committed to Ettingshall and live in the ward. Your Labour Team's most recent achievements include:

▶ Improved council housing with double glazing and central heating
▶ The new market way and Sure Start crèche and nursery centre of excellence
▶ Better education achievement for our children

▶ Delivering recycling and tackling litter on our streets
▶ Working to improve community safety

Andrew and Alan have served the City as a whole as Cabinet member for Environmental Services and Chair of the Licensing Panel respectively. As leading members they know how to make things happen.

Working through the Bilston Area Forum and local community groups your Labour Team gives its promise to continue to work to improve Ettingshall for your benefit. They will continue to be available at regular advice surgeries, on the phone, or by regular 'Down Your Way' visits.

use all your **VOTES** for **LABOUR**

vote
Labour

your**LABOUR**candidates

Printed By Clarity Print, Electrium Point, Forge Road, Willenhall, WV12 4HD
Promoted by Peter Davies, 44 Shale Street, Bilston WV14 0HF
On behalf of the Labour party candidates for Ettingshall Ward all at 44 Shale Street, Bilston WV14 0HF

organisations were doing most valuable work, providing many useful services to the community. I would like to mention some of the most significant such organisations which were delivering specialised quality services in the most deprived section of the community here in Wolverhampton. There are the Haque Centre and the Sewa Centre.

THE SAGA OF THE HAQUE CENTRE
(A welfare advice Centre)

A large number of migrant populations came to the United Kingdom during the period of the Sixties and Seventies using employment vouchers issued by the British government. Many of them, especially from the Indian sub-continent came to Wolverhampton because they had friends or relatives living here already. The majority of them were unable to read, write or speak English and on arrival here in this strange land of hope and glory they were faced with multiple problems such as housing, employment, welfare benefits, passports and immigration status and much more. There was no help or support easily available where they could go to access information and guidance on this complicated matter. People used to rely on friends or relatives for help and support in filling in the forms and their children would often act as interpreters. These arrangements were far from satisfactory and often proved inadequate to deal with complicated legal documents.

In 1982, some of us from the local community organised ourselves and set up a charitable organization in the name of All Saints Hague Centre. We decided to find a suitable venue in All Saints, one of the most deprived inner city areas of Wolverhampton. The aims and objects of this centre were to provide badly needed services of advice, information and guidance in welfare rights, social security, housing, immigration, nationality and many more topics. The Hague Centre was set up at 23 Vicarage Road in All Saints, in a terraced house rented from the local authority. I managed to persuade the Council to provide the necessary grant funding for a full time advice worker and secretarial support and

249

to pay for the overheads.

The centre became extremely popular with people from the black and ethnic minorities and responded positively to the increased demand from the local community seeking help and support. We were successful in getting more financial support from various sources to employ more advisers to meet the increasing demand for our services.

The Centre developed into a reasonably large organization within a few years and moved into larger offices at 25/27 Vicarage Road, and eventually opened another centre in a different part of the city. At one time, we were employing more than twenty full and part-time workers and dealing with over twenty thousand clients a year. Due to the quality of its services the Centre gained popularity not only in the city of Wolverhampton but also much further afield throughout the whole Midlands. The Hague Centre served the community for more than 23 years providing a most needed and valuable service.

Unfortunately, the centre closed down in 2006 due to some management problems and the community lost a most valuable asset for forever. Once again, the evil of caste hatred and religious prejudice took a toll in the running of the Centre. Its manager, Jaswant Chandel, and another senior worker, Ghan Sham Saini, became victims of caste discrimination. The management committee of the Haque Centre led by Mr Bangey and Mr Satpal, the secretary, treated them unfairly and hounded them out of their jobs for no reason other than caste prejudice. The Centre lost its funding, workers lost their livelihood and the people of Wolverhampton lost valuable services that would be extremely difficult to reinstate.

Jaswant Chandel ,the manager of the Haque Centre and his fellow colleague, Ghan Sham Saini, took their cases to an Industrial Tribunal in Birmingham. I stood as a witness for both of them, giving evidence of racial hatred on the basis of caste and religion. The three defendants, Dilbag Bangey, SatPal and The Hague Centre, brought in a number of witnesses in their defence. It was a lengthy hearing lasting more than two weeks. I submitted a written statement of five pages and stood in the witness box for almost two days. At the end of the hearing, the presiding judge in his forty page judgment commended me as credible and trustworthy witness. All three respondents were found guilty of racial prejudice based on caste and religion, unfair treatment and victimisation. They were fined heavily and were required to pay the legal costs.

This case was of special significance as this was for the first time that an incident of racial prejudice based on Indian caste and religion was tried and proved in an United Kingdom court under the 2005 Equality Act. Many legal practitioners had since used this case for reference in courts.

BIRTH OF SEWA CENTRE

After the closure of the Hague Centre, a huge gap was left in services such as information, advice and guidance on welfare rights, council tax, housing, immigration, nationality and many more topics. People were extremely concerned about the loss of most of these valuable services which made help and support readily available free of charge on their doorstep.

There was a grassroots campaign and a strong lobby from local residents demanding reinstatement of the services as soon as possible. It was impossible even to think of setting up another advice centre like the Hague Centre—there was no hope of any funding available due to local government budget cuts. However, in spite of all the uncertainties of funding, I was encouraged by Jaswant Chancel to do something in response to the demands of local residents. He asked my help and support in finding a suitable building in the All Saints area to set up an office. He had an idea to organise and run an advice centre with the help of volunteers. The office building at 48/50 Vicarage Road, previously used by the Haque Centre was readily available and we approached the owner and managed to persuade him to let us use it free of charge for some time until we could organise some funding. Mr Chandel and some of his colleagues (all previous employees of the Hague Centre) agreed to work as volunteers in order to open the office for a few hours a week to provide a limited service.

We struggled to run the office for eighteen months on small grants from various sources to pay for the overheads. During this time, we organised a proper management committee and registered it as a charitable limited company. In order to make the project sustainable we started exploring longer-term financial backing from various different avenues including grant funding from sources like the Big Lottery. Our application for Big Lottery Funding was successful and we were awarded £400 000 for three year to employ six full time workers. It was like dream come true, and this news brought great relief and joy to every one involved including the local community.

We had huge compliments and were widely commended for our good work in bringing such a large amount of money to the city, creating jobs and providing a most needed service to the residents. Mr Chandel and I worked hard during the Christmas holiday period of 2010 on setting up the office, fixing furniture, arranging for phone and internet lines to be installed and preparing to recruit staff.

The Sewa Centre had a strong team of seven dedicated members of the management committee with a wealth of expertise in different fields of life. The committee provided every possible help and support to enhance the work of the Centre and the staff and the management committee worked together for three years to meet the targets and achieve the outcomes to comply with the funding conditions. The success of the Centre provided us with a springboard and strengthened our case for further grant funding from the Big Lottery.

We started developing a fresh application for funding from the beginning of 2013 and submitted it to the Big Lottery. There was a delay about the outcome of our application due to a large number of applications compared with previous years. It was a race against time as we were reaching the end of our existing funding period. The management committee and the staff, every one were awaiting the outcome of our application. With no news forthcoming, however, the management committee considered plans to close the office, issue redundancy notices to staff and surrender the tenancy of the office building. By the end of November 2013, we saw our hopes of further funding appearing to fade away day by day. Then all of a sudden, there seemed to be light at the end of the tunnel and good news was in sight. Despite tough competition due to cuts and the third sector losing grant funding from local authorities our application was approved.

Once again, our application for Big Lottery funding was successful and again the Sewa Centre had grant funding of £400,000 to employ six full time workers. It came at a time when everybody was going through tough times to comply with demands for budget cuts imposed by the central government. Once again, this news for funding brought great joy all over and congratulations for everyone involved with Sewa Centre.

The new project funded by the Big Lottery Funding is now operational and providing a most valuable service. We are now having an increased number of clients coming to the Centre for help and support due to several organisations providing similar facilities closing down due to cuts in funding.

It gives me great pleasure and I feel proud to be a member and chair of the Sewa Centre. This gives me inner satisfaction to see so many people coming to the centre seeking help to deal with their problems. I feel proud when people stop me to thank me for setting up a Centre where they can access services that suit their individual needs.

Pat McFadden MP visited the Sewa Centre sitting with me on the front. Standing behind are board members Sehdev Bismal MB, M.L. Sharma. Councillor Elias Mattu, and on the right Jaswant Chandel, manager of the centre together with the rest of the staff.

NIRVANA

"Pride vs Prejudice" is not a story of just my life; it is a story of millions who had been through or are the subject of prejudice, oppression and discriminatory treatment on this beautiful planet earth. I salute all those who had sacrificed their lives fighting for the cause of equality, liberty, justice and peace. I often think about what I was and what I am now, who I was and who am I now, where I come from and what I have achieved in my life. I have been able to achieve some positive results and do things beyond my own imagination despite endless barriers, discrimination, opposition and prejudice. All the personal abuse, insults, intimidation and threats in my personal life have helped strengthen my resolve and determination and have never deterred or diverted my attention. Often I think whether it is due to sheer circumstances, my own relentless efforts or prevailing opportunities that I have been able to serve the community and contribute to bring about changes for the better. I am pleased and indeed proud to have been able to contribute though in a small way to the agenda of equality and fairness in society.

Over the past half a century I have seen many changes taking place all over the world—the Union of Soviet Socialist Republics disintegrated, the partition of independent India into Bangladesh, India and Pakistan, the unification of East and West Germany to mention but a few. Science and technology have revolutionised our lives—the whole world witnessed humans landing on moon in 1969, the invention of social media and internet has brought the international community ever closer. Things around the world may be changing faster changes in discrimination and prejudice around the world seem to be negligible.

When I came to England, after landing at Heathrow Airport I found myself helpless as there was no one to receive me. I was extremely worried as I have nowhere to go and had only three pounds in my pocket. It gives me a great pleasure and consolation that I have been able to help many in need. It makes me feel proud when people pass compliments and say thank you for your help and support. It gives me huge pleasure when I see thousands of people using the Sewa Centre for information, advice and guidance. All these compliments, respect and affection are a source of great pride in my life and resonate my feelings as if I had attained NIRVANA in life.

People all over the world are looking for happiness and satisfaction in life. Some people are trying to find happiness through huge wealth, big business, a large beautiful house whilst other take to alcohol, drugs and gambling. Others, like me achieve it through helping others especially those who are less fortunate than others.

My grand mother used to say that a guest to your house is like a god; to serve and make him happy is equal to offering your devotions and services to please the God. I had learned and inherited from my elders the qualities of being helpful and serving others in need. All these qualities give great pleasure, eternal happiness and satisfaction and this is the NIRVANA of my life. Prime minister Harold Wilson resigned suddenly on 16th March 1976, surprising the whole world. Press reporters asked him the reason for his resignation and he modestly replied, 'I have been MP for 31 years, minister for 13 years and Prime Minister for eight years'. What else does a person need in life? One should not ask for more'" This was an excellent expression of self-satisfaction.

I would like to thank most sincerely all those who have continuously encouraged me and provided me with all possible help and support to make my life a success and to achieve NIRVANA.

EVERY PICTURE TELLS A STORY

There is a famous saying that says that a picture is worth a thousand words and on that basis I will finish this book with a gallery of photographs, every one of which tells its own story.

And finally, a photograph taken at the National Arts & Museums Conference in Guernsey in September 1984 at which I represented Wolverhampton.